Gay Hendricks is a psychologist and professor at the University of Colorado. He is the author of ten books in the fields of psychology and education, including *The Centered Teacher, The Family Centering Book,* and *The Centered Athlete.*

Kathlyn Hendricks is a registered dance-movement therapist who has been in private practice for more than ten years. The author of many articles in her field, she lectures and gives workshops in the U.S. and abroad. Her major interest is in integrating transpersonal psychology and movement.

Prentice-Hall International, Inc., *London*
Prentice-Hall of Australia Pty. Limited, *Sydney*
Prentice-Hall Canada Inc., *Toronto*
Prentice-Hall of India Private Limited, *New Delhi*
Prentice-Hall of Japan, Inc., *Tokyo*
Prentice-Hall of Southeast Asia Pte. Ltd., *Singapore*
Whitehall Books Limited, *Wellington, New Zealand*
Editora Prentice-Hall do Brasil Ltda., *Rio de Janeiro*

The moving center

EXPLORING MOVEMENT ACTIVITIES FOR THE CLASSROOM

Gay & Kathlyn Hendricks

A SPECTRUM BOOK

Prentice-Hall, Inc., Englewood Cliffs, New Jersey 07632

Library of Congress Cataloging in Publication Data

Hendricks, Gay.
    The moving center.

    "A Spectrum Book."
    Bibliography: p.
    Includes index.
    1. Movement education.   I. Hendricks, Kathlyn.
II. Title.
GV452.H46 1983   372.8'6   83-11008
ISBN 0-13-604322-4
ISBN 0-13-604314-3 (pbk.)

GV
452
H46
1983

For Chris and Gabriel

1 2 3 4 5 6 7 8 9 10

ISBN 0-13-604322-4
ISBN 0-13-604314-3 {PBK.}

Editorial/production supervision and interior design by Carol Smith
Cover design by Ben Santora
Interior illustrations by Missye Bonds
Manufacturing buyer: Doreen Cavallo

This book is available at a special discount
when ordered in bulk quantities.
Contact Prentice-Hall, Inc., General Publishing Division,
Special Sales, Englewood Cliffs, N.J. 07632.

Contents

Exploring
the transpersonal realm 75

Exploring time 85

Exploring space 93

Exploring weight 101

I would like to acknowledge the invaluable assistance of Jack Downing, who gently suggested that I learn to dance. My deep gratitude goes also to Amanda and Kathlyn for dancing with me in ways that made everything worthwhile.

—*Gay Hendricks*

The activities in this book are based on the contributions of many students and colleagues. This book has grown from the nourishment of many dance-movement therapists dedicated to the unfolding joy of movement and the drive toward wholeness. I am especially grateful to Mary Whitehouse for opening the path from the body to the spirit, to Joan Chodorow for teaching me to trust the natural process, to Patricia Burbank for demonstrating such creative zest and for germinating several of the activities, and to Judith Bell for contributing to the outline of the translation process.

—*Kathlyn Hendricks*

THE MOVING CENTER

Becoming
a moving teacher

As teachers, we want our students to be all that they can be. Just as we are grateful to the teachers who put us in touch with powers we did not know we had, so we now hope to assist our students in feeling and expressing the full range of their potential, not only intellectually but also physically, emotionally, and spiritually. We come into teaching with a desire to touch students in ways that have lasting positive consequences.

To do this, we must communicate with the whole of our own being, and that of our students; we teach who we are, not just what we know. In their fullest form, teaching and learning are done with our whole bodies, not just the tiny part of us we call the intellect. For those teachers who wish to speak with the whole person, movement is the voice.

Why Use Movement in Teaching?

Our world, especially as children, is charged with sensory experience. Each person is heir to a many-million-year legacy of refinement in feeling, seeing, touching, tasting, and smelling. Each of us has inherited a capacity for the pure joy of moving through space, of exploring the inner and outer worlds. We live in bodies that want to move. But as we go along in life, many of us encounter conventions and conditioning that tell us to stop moving. Somewhere we learn that our celebration of the joy of movement must be stifled in order to join the "grown-up" world.

Sound education strikes a balance between conscious mental activity and conscious movement. Sadly, movement is often limited to physical education class and the slow shuffle from classroom to classroom. There are many negative consequences of denying the body's need to move and learn about itself. Ignored, the body stiffens, decreasing its capacity for feeling. Ignored for too long, it falls prey to degenerative diseases. Unless the body is tended and celebrated, it cannot be used for its full potential of joy and learning.

Another reason for using movement in teaching is to. bring people more in harmony with themselves and others. Moving together is a superb way of building community. We all know the unpleasant effects of the lack of a sense of community, whether in a classroom or in the world at large. There is something about dancing and moving with one's fellows that can dissolve the stiffness and alienation that sometimes occur between humans. In a classroom, teacher and students moving together can build the kind of rapport that is at the heart of meaningful education.

Too, movement is a path to deeper levels of experience. Much schooling tiptoes around the intellectual periphery of life. As the poet William Blake put it, "Energy is the only life, and is from the body; and reason is the bound or outward circumference of energy. Energy is eternal delight." Once we break through the thin crust of intellect, we have access to a richer and more delightful fare than we may ever have dreamed possible . . . feeling, sensation, the myriad hums and buzzes of a world of tumbling energy. Education generally focuses on what and how we think. Kept in perspective, this mental focus is valuable; but if it deludes us into denigrating feeling and the life of the body, then it does us little good.

Movement can prevent many of the common problems that plague the classroom. Disruptive behavior, for example, often is the result of an imbalance between sitting and moving. By integrating movement experiences into the activities of the classroom, the teacher can head off many disruptions before they occur. In the same vein, we now are more knowledgeable about individual learning styles. Some people are visual learners, some are auditory, and some are kinesthetic. Given the same learning task, some children will get it best through pictures, some will get it best through words and sounds, and some will get it best through body experiences. In addition, all of us, no matter how strong our auditory or visual parts are, have a kinesthetic part within us that needs to be served. Kinesthetic learners have typically gotten the short end of the slide rule in schooling. Whereas there is plenty of talk in schools, and more recently plenty of audio-visual aids, there certainly are very few kinesthetic aids to bring out the feeling and moving parts of ourselves.

Finally, there is a lesson to be learned from exploring the body that can be crucial to our subsequent development. This lesson is that the body doesn't lie. Many people become unhappy and ill each year because they do not learn to listen to what their bodies are telling them. Many others do not make the most of their lives because they have not tuned in to the directions in which their bodies want to take them. Sadly, the process of growing up often involves a split between mind and body so that they do battle with each other. The body is coughing out a "stop smoking" message, while the mind is saying, "I smoke for pleasure." The body says "rest me," the mind drives it on to an accident. The body becomes full of tension, the mind does not inquire into what might be causing it. If we do not begin early in life to prevent this split, much more effort must go into remedying it later on. So, movement exploration can be regarded as being an essential form of preventive medicine that can enhance the quality of life at the moment of doing it and long, long after.

The Objectives of
Movement Exploration

There are two major areas of objectives in doing movement work in education: cognitive and affective, that which can be known and that which can be felt. Let's consider each briefly.

COGNITIVE OBJECTIVES   All teachers must be on the lookout at all times for innovative strategies to teach the cogni-

5

tive material at hand, whether it be math, literature, or woodworking. Movement offers a new way of conceptualizing the cognitive objectives in education. Once we get comfortable with the notion of using the whole body in teaching, new vistas open up. The teacher who has previously taught subtraction to her or his second-graders using a chalkboard can now enhance the lesson with a movement game in which the children form different-sized groups, subtract themselves, and count the remainders.

Movement gives students permission to use all their senses in learning. We do not know enough about the learning process to insist that children only use intellectual processes. Anything we can do to help children expand into learning with the full range of themselves can have a high payoff.

Movement bridges mind and body, enabling us to integrate new information into ourselves. Many of us have had the experience of being exposed to new data in a traditional way—through explanations, examples, and diagrams—only to "get it" later when we're taking a walk or playing marbles. Movement often has the effect of bringing mental learning down into the body so that we have a whole-body understanding of it.

Movement is universal. As teachers, we are always seeking ways of putting abstract notions into concrete examples so that our students can relate to them. Since nearly all of us can relate to movement, it becomes a new way of making abstractions concrete once we learn to use it.

The recent research on right- and left-brain functions suggests that a better balance could be achieved in education between intellectual activities and right-hemisphere functions such as spatial relations, metaphor, dreams, and music. Movement takes us out of the logic-dominated left hemisphere and puts us more in touch with the body and its energy.

AFFECTIVE OBJECTIVES Most teachers would agree that there are certain key affective objectives that should be part of every classroom, no matter whether in elementary school or college. Movement exploration can present affective lessons in ways that are interesting and fun.

Many adults complain of being out of touch with their feelings and needs. Much time and energy are spent later in life trying to become aware of who we are, how we really feel, what we really want. One of the biggest services a teacher can provide is to give students experiences that connect them with their inner sensations, feelings, and needs. These types of learning will often be remembered and used long after the niceties of the past perfect subjunctive and the quadratic equation have been forgotten. In one way or another, every movement activity in this book can help us to be more aware of inner experience.

Another major affective objective is creativity. One problem that many people feel is a lack of contact with the spontaneous creative energy within them. Over time, many of us shut off the channel that connects us with our creativity. One of the major advantages of doing movement work is that it can reopen that channel. The activities in this book give people the opportunity to find the place in themselves from which spontaneous creative activity emerges. Once we have learned to find and nurture that place, we are more likely to keep an open and friendly relationship with it.

One of the main affective goals in life is the integration of the many polarities within us: good/bad, should/shouldn't, right/wrong, one/many, love/hate. For example, many of us struggle to come into harmony with the strong/weak polarity; we want to be strong so that we can carry out purposeful, successful action, and we want to be open and vulnerable so that we have access to the tender parts of ourselves and others. Movement is the means by which polarities are most readily manifested to our awareness and explored. By learning how polarities make themselves known through the body and its movement, we can be aware of many of the disturbing splits in ourselves.

Self-concept is a fundamental affective objective. How we feel about ourselves is grounded in our body image. There are many components to a successful self-concept; one essential is flexibility, another is confidence, still another, the ability to have direct and immediate access to the truth of one's experience. All of these components are enhanced through the exploration of movement. There are mental and emotional factors that play a role in self-concept also; these too can be developed through the use of movement. For example, one's ability to solve problems, which on the surface seems a purely mental ability, can actually be improved through learning more about body movement. (Chapter 6 provides excellent problem-solving activities.)

One of the greatest affective objectives, one that can lead to lifelong enrichment, is the development of an inner life. Teachers can make lasting contributions by putting their students in touch with the deep and nourishing flow of experience within them. There are magnificent vistas of interior life that are available to us: dreams, feelings, needs, songs, dance. Also within is a symphony of body experience, the streaming wisdom of millions of years of evolution. Movement is a way of gaining access to the inner treasure trove we all share.

In a complex and rapidly changing world, we can greatly benefit from having a growing relationship with the part of us that is always with us—our innermost sense of being. Whether we call it spirit or essence or soul, it is that part of us that is deeply and directly connected to the timeless. This spirit lives through the body; movement nurtures it, keeping it alive and growing.

For thousands of years, people have been moving and dancing together as a way of finding a rapport and a sense of community with each other. In many societies, dance is a high form of celebration, used in weddings, births, and other rites of passage. In western society, movement has been deemphasized as a celebration. We do not dance our Thanksgiving; we eat together or watch football. A new father does not organize a birth dance for the others in the community; cigars are dispensed instead. Movement is catching on again, however. At first, it is segregated into specialized places such as rock clubs and the jogging path. One of the enduring affective objectives we can offer our students is to let them know how to build movement rituals into their daily lives. That way, movement will again be woven into the fabric of life, and we will become as fluent in speaking the language of the body as we are in vocal speech.

2

Beginning to move

This chapter introduces the use of movement activities in your learning environment. We will offer some suggestions based on our experiences, then take you through four experiments that are representative of the fifty-two activities you will find as you go through the book.

There is a short introduction to each activity to define its goal and give suggestions to you, the leader. This is followed by instructions that have been written to be read verbatim to the group. Please do not feel limited by our suggestions or our words. We hope you will feel free to improvise and create new variations on the themes we have suggested. As you discover your own additions and changes, we suggest that you note them in the margins so that you will have all the information you need in one place.

Some of the materials you might want to assemble to facilitate the activities are:

- material remnants: excellent for improvisation, making costumes or structures, hiding behind, and so on
- stretch ropes: available from surplus or marine stores; can be used individually or in pairs or groups to define body boundaries, invent games
- drop cloths: get the thinnest kind; under supervision, great fun for group interaction, costumes, movement exploration, sensory integration
- balloons: get the strongest kind; endless inventions possible, great for stretch break or warm-up
- percussion instruments: anyone can play and be expressive
- pastels and butcher paper: end rolls are usually free from your local newspaper; useful in many activities
- costumes: easy to collect from thrift stores; good for fairy tales, dream work, fantasy, role playing
- newspapers: a great way, when wadded and thrown, to release tension safely; people *love* it
- bubble solution and wands: to lighten things up, teach qualities of flow and lightness
- feathers: for relaxation, tactile awareness
- stuffed animals and puppets: a place for students to put their feelings and fantasies.

There are several attitudes that have been found useful in making movement exploration easier and more fun. First, it is perfectly all right to make mistakes. There are no right

or wrong answers in movement exploration—the goal is simply the joy of learning. If you can master this attitude and foster it in your students, the activities will be a much greater source of enjoyment. Second, you don't have to be a dancer or know anything about dance to be successful with movement activities. Some of the most profound learnings grow out of experiences with people who swear they can't dance. Everyone can benefit from learning more about the body and how it moves. Third, take some time to tune your own instrument and those of the group with which you are working. Take a stretch break to limber up your body, do some deep breathing to fill the body with energy, acknowledge how you are feeling at the moment— in short, do anything you can do to help yourself and your group warm up and feel more comfortable. Fourth, and perhaps most important, give yourself and the group permission to have fun. Nobody ever said learning had to be dull. Movement can make the driest subject absolutely exhilarating.

Now on to the experiments.

BODY PARTS DANCE

TO THE LEADER   This experiment explores body awareness while giving participants a chance to feel more alive and share in the joy of moving.

The choice of music for this experiment is important. It is a playful activity and can be enhanced by fun music such as honky-tonk, New Orleans jazz, or carnival music. Students may be seated, standing by their desks, or in a circle.

INSTRUCTIONS TO THE GROUP   I'm going to put on some music, and we're going to focus on moving different body parts in all the ways we can think of. During this activity, feel free to look around and get ideas from the way others are moving. I'll start by calling out a part.

(Start music; allow approximately 1 minute for each part.)

Shoulders . . . let your shoulders lead your movement up . . . around . . . hunched . . . high . . . wiggling. Now chins . . . how can you move your chin? . . . jutting . . . snooty . . . drooping . . . let your whole body follow your chin. Now you can call out different parts and we'll focus on that part.

(*Continue for 3 or 4 minutes.*)

Now move any part of you that wants to move . . . and now slow down until you are at a good stopping place, then sit down.

FLYING FREE

TO THE LEADER Movement is like a radar screen on which you can see the passing thoughts and images of the mind, the emotions and sensations of the body. The blips and tracks are similar to the passing selves and roles we wear; the screen itself represents our underlying unity of self.

It is only when we hold onto or try to fix these passing blips that we encounter problems such as tension, unhappiness, and lack of satisfying contact with others. This activity can remind participants that life is a continual flow of events, feelings, and interactions, and that satisfaction comes from enjoying the dance rather than holding onto the moment.

This activity can be done in a circle or with students randomly spaced throughout the room. A circle provides more structure and gives students an opportunity to see others easily. Random spacing of children uses the normal arrangement of many classrooms.

You will need a drum or a tambourine.

INSTRUCTIONS TO THE GROUP   I'm going to beat the drum in an eight-count beat: four counts loud—BOOM BOOM BOOM BOOM—and four counts soft—Boom Boom Boom Boom. I'll start slowly, then I might increase the speed later.

On the strong beats, freeze your body into a sculpture that says HERE I AM! On the soft beats, breathe and let your body melt and come unglued. Then on the next strong beats, freeze into another sculpture that says HERE I AM!

Hold . . . BOOM BOOM BOOM BOOM . . . Melt . . . Boom Boom Boom Boom.

(*Repeat 5–10 times.*)

Now we'll try some other positions. Again, hold the sculpture on the strong beats, then melt and dissolve on the soft beats.

(*Repeat each of the following 3–4 times.*)

- I'm big . . . BOOM BOOM BOOM BOOM Boom Boom Boom Boom
- I'm lovable . . . BOOM BOOM BOOM BOOM Boom Boom Boom Boom
- I'm capable . . . BOOM BOOM BOOM BOOM Boom Boom Boom Boom
- I can do it . . . BOOM BOOM BOOM BOOM Boom Boom Boom Boom.

VARIATIONS   Have the students jump and change the sculpture each time they land.

Have them dissolve all the way to the floor.

Ask them to take on sculptures that look like people in their family or TV characters.

FLYING FREE—DUETS

TO THE LEADER   This experiment follows the same theme as the previous activity while adding a new dimension. It gives participants an opportunity to listen actively with their bodies and introduces the skills of interacting with others through movement.

INSTRUCTIONS TO THE GROUP   Choose a partner and stand facing each other. Decide who will be Partner One and Partner Two.

Partner One, find a way of standing that most looks like how you feel when you are solid as a rock or a mountain. Do it now, making your body very big and solid, and hold that position as long as you can.

Partner Two, take the same position as your partner is doing. Try it on in your body—head, elbows, back, feet, everywhere—and notice how it feels in your body.

Great! Both partners, shake out your arms and legs and let go of that position.

(*Repeat with Partner Two leading.*)

Now, Partner One, again let your body become solid as a mountain. Hold onto that position as long as you can. Then when you're ready, totally melt down, let go of the position, and let your body fly free. Move around however you want. Partner Two, when Partner One melts, it's your turn to take the position. Keep switching back and forth. When one melts and flies free, it's the other's turn to take the position.

VARIATIONS   Try these positions:

- feeling good about yourself
- feeling scared
- feeling at home, knowing you belong here
- a position that says, "Right now I feel _____."

Imagine

- you're a race car frozen in the middle of a turn
- a way you meet people: shyly, loudly, confidently
- the way you stand when you're talking to other students . . . to older people . . . to your parents.

19

DOMINOES

The purpose of this activity is to continue the process of increasing flexibility that was begun in the previous experiments.

Your primary task in the activity is to tap the beginning domino when the group is ready. This experiment involves the whole group in the letting-go process and is best done in a circle. Later you may devise other patterns such as letters, shapes, or numbers.

INSTRUCTIONS TO THE GROUP   Form a circle with enough room around you to swing your arms. Now everyone freeze. Hold your body in a sculpture that says HERE I AM!

Now glance around without moving your head, and notice everyone's position.

In a moment I'm going to tap one of you. When I do, begin to melt and ooze out of your position into a puddle on the floor. When you ooze all the way onto the floor, that will be a signal to the person next to you to start melting down, too. When that person dissolves onto the floor, the next person starts melting. Any questions?

Let's do it totally in silence. You can make faces and soundless yells, but nothing we can hear.

(*Tap the first person.*)

VARIATIONS   Try different positions:

- I'm shy
- I'm fierce

- See me!
- I'm hiding.

Try to see how fast the dominoes can melt. How slowly. Go in random order rather than one person after the next.

Exploring feelings through movement

Perhaps the most central lesson in affective education is learning to come into harmony with our feelings. Learning to feel, learning how to tell one feeling from another, and learning how to express feelings clearly are all examples of the types of learning that can have very powerful consequences in school and later in life.

Consistent with the whole-person approach to learning emphasized in this book, the experiments in this chapter are examples of the ways that movement can be used to explore feelings.

FLUFFING

TO THE LEADER Daily stress can flatten our bodies and our capacity for feeling fully alive. Fluffing is designed to reacquaint us with our internal feeling of lightness.

INSTRUCTIONS TO THE GROUP Wherever you are in the room right now, standing or sitting, take a few moments to close your eyes.

Imagine that your breath is a soft, swirling cloud of relaxation. Each time you breathe in, send the cloud to a different part of your body to fluff it. As you breathe out let that part gently float through the space around you. First fluff up under your shoulders . . . fluff up as you would fluff a pillow . . . under your shoulder blades . . . between your ribs . . . in your belly . . . behind your knees. Now breathe the cloud into your whole body at the same time, fluffing everywhere. Breathe out, enjoying the lightness.

A FEELING KALEIDOSCOPE

TO THE LEADER Everyone has feelings, all kinds of feelings. The body is a feeling machine, containing joy, anger, fear, sadness, and dozens of other emotional experiences. If we are not acquainted with our feelings, they can run us. If we are willing to experience feelings and be at home with them, we can feel a deep sense of mastery over ourselves.

This activity is like the game we used to play called "Chinese Firedrill"; when our car came to a halt at a stoplight, everyone would jump out, run around the car, and then jump back in, changing seats. In this experiment, feeling changes are introduced as rapidly as that.

Music is particularly useful for this activity. Some suggestions to convey various moods follow (for others, consult the list in the *References*).

25

Exploring feelings through movement

- *Joy:* Holst, *The Planets,* "Mars"; Reich, *Music for 18 Musicians;* Rampal and Bolling, *Suite for Flute and Jazz Piano*
- *Anger:* Olatunji, *Drums of Passion;* Orff, *Carmina Burana;* Eno and Byrne, *My Life in the Bush of Ghosts*
- *Sadness:* Rodrigo, *Concierto de Aranjuez,* "Adagio"; Messiaen, *Quartet for the End of Time;* Hadjidakis, *Lilacs Out of the Dead Land*
- *Fear:* Wolff and Hennings, *Tibetan Bells I and II;* Deuter, *Haleakala,* "Haleakala Mystery."

INSTRUCTIONS TO THE GROUP   Choose a place in the room. Each time I play music, let your arms and legs paint a feeling in the air around you. When the music stops, become very still and open inside. We will switch from one feeling to another quite rapidly.

Rest for a moment in your place . . . let your body become very still.

(Begin sad music.)

Let your toes and feet move sadly through the room, shuffling along . . . sighing feet, sad feet. Let sadness creep up through you until all of you is sad. Let your arms move in a sad way.

(Continue for 1–2 minutes.)

Now come to rest.

(Begin angry music.)

Let your fingers and hands move angrily . . . grumbling, irritated, mad hands. Now let the rest of you be mad, too. Be a big, puffing locomotive of anger.

(*Continue for 1 minute.*)

Now come to rest.

(*Begin scared music.*)

Now let yourself be scared. Find a way to make your body scared . . . hide it from the world . . . hold your breath high up under your shoulders and move scared . . . creep around the room.

(*Continue for 1 minute.*)

Now come to rest.

(*Begin joyful music.*)

Now let everything be *great!* Let your head move as though you just found out you were going to Disneyland. Let your whole body be happy. Celebrate yourself!

(*Continue 1–2 minutes or longer.*)

Now come to rest.

VARIATIONS   Try expressing different feelings:

- *Irritation:* Move as though a fly keeps landing on you.
- *Confusion:* Move your body in three directions at once, as though each is pulling on you. Let the feeling of confusion move through you.

- *Depression:* Let your chest move as though a heavy weight is pulling it down to the floor. Drag yourself along, heavy and depressed.
- *Grumpiness:* Make your chin and elbows and fists say "I'm grumpy today," and "don't mess with me."
- *Being off-balance:* Move as though you can't find your balance. You can't find the middle of you, the center place. Let your legs and body keep taking you off balance.

Try different structures. Move the feelings through very quickly, changing every 10–15 seconds.

Use the image of a box that students can come out of moving to a certain feeling. When they go back into the box, it's rest time.

TALKING WITH YOUR BODY—TELEPHONE

TO THE LEADER   Learning to listen to the messages of the body can build lifelong sources of discovery and renewal. Health and creativity are based in open channels between mind and body. This experiment is about making friends with our inner selves, and is the basis for more complex experiments we shall do with feelings.

Try this experiment with lights dimmed and non-rhythmic background music set at a soft tone to help students relax.

28

INSTRUCTIONS TO THE GROUP   Ooze your body down into a place on the floor . . . all the way down. Breathe in all the way to the top, and whoosh, all at once breathe out through your mouth. Close your eyes and breathe in again to the top and all the way out. Let your body wiggle as fast as you can.

(*Hold for 15 seconds.*)

Now rest and sink down into the floor. Let your ears become very large to hear an imaginary telephone ringing. The telephone is ringing in your right hand; listen with your insides to hear what your hand has to say. It might say, "I'm wiggly and excited"; it might say, "I'm tired and want to hold something." Let it begin to move just the way it wants to move. Moving is one way your body talks to you.

Now let the telephone ring in your left foot. Pick up the phone by letting your foot move *just the way it feels* . . . listen with all of you as your foot talks . . . big movements . . . tiny movements . . . the way your foot is right now.

Now let the telephone ring where your body feels most tight. What does this tight place have to say? Let your body listen to the way the tight place wants to move. Ask yourself what you need, and listen to the moving.

Let the telephone ring someplace in your body, wherever you hear it. Does it ring very loudly, or can you barely hear it? Allow that part to talk to you, to say anything it wishes.

Now rest and take a moment to remember whether your body needs anything from you. Take a breath that says, I love you; I'm willing to talk with you. When you feel awake and alert, open your eyes, stretch, and get up.

VARIATIONS Let the telephone ring in different body parts: back of the neck, eyelids, ankles, behind the knees, belly, inside the elbow.

Let the telephone ring in a part of your body where you feel sad . . . in your most relaxed part . . . in a part of you that you really like . . . where you feel confused.

After a little practice, students can do this seated at their desks as well as lying down. This experiment is a good warm-up before going on to other movement exploration.

FINDING THE YES AND NO PLACES

TO THE LEADER Knowing what we like and dislike, what we most deeply want and don't want, is part of *meta*learning, learning about how we learn. Taking responsibility can be vital and exciting when we can identify impulses that are truest to our deepest nature. In this experiment, we've found that saying no often opens the possibility of saying yes.

This experiment can be quite noisy.

INSTRUCTIONS TO THE GROUP Find your place in a circle. Take a moment to look around and see everyone. We're going to take turns saying no, listening to all the different ways we say no. Say a big no. I'll begin.

(Make eye contact with each person as he or she says no.)

Now let's go around again. This time, let your arms and legs and face say no along with your voice. Make it *bigger* than everyday.

(Go around the circle a couple of times in quick succession.)

Pause a moment and notice your body. Now move around the room, repeating no in all the ways you can, and feel where the no starts in you. If you see someone else's no that looks like fun, try it on too. Where is your no place?

(Continue for 2–3 minutes.)

Now quickly find a partner and stand facing each other. Take turns letting your whole body say no to each other. Let your body be a big drum that booms no!

(Continue for 1–2 minutes.)

Now keep saying no, but without words. Take turns letting no out your fingers and back and feet.

(1–2 minutes.)

Now one of you keep saying no with your body and the other one start saying yes with your body. A yes–no conversation. Say yes just as big as you said no.

(2 minutes.)

Now switch. If you were saying yes, now be a huge no. If you were no, begin finding your yes place.

Exploring feelings through movement

(1–2 minutes.)

Everyone now move around the room again saying yes, sometimes out loud and sometimes just with your body. Where is that place in you that feels, "All right! Go for it!"? Your feeling good about yourself place? Let the movement start there.

(2 minutes.)

Come back into the circle now and let's go around once more, sharing our yes with each other. Let all of you say yes!

COMMENT Discussion of this experiment is often very useful to share students' insights about which expression was easier. Questions and comments that might come up include: Is saying no bad? I love saying no, but I couldn't find a yes place; when my partner said no, I forgot about saying yes; saying no was so much *fun*, is that okay?

Assisting students in claiming their internal experience and expression of this fundamental feeling cycle can lead to a deeper sense of acceptance of all feelings and the decisions that emerge from them.

Building positive self-concept

How we feel about ourselves is a foundation for everything we do. At the source, all of the activities in education are potential self-concept builders, for to teach a student to subtract in a culture that uses subtraction is to give that student a skill that carries with it a positive feeling about the self. In this chapter, however, we approach the self directly. We explore who we are and how we feel about ourselves, not through the medium of a cognitive skill but through our bodies and our movement.

The self-concept is as inevitably rooted in our bodies as it is in our minds. For this reason, these activities can be quite powerful. We encourage plenty of reflection and discussion time when you do these experiments.

MOVING THROUGH LIFE

TO THE LEADER   In this experiment, participants can see themselves in new ways and perhaps see themselves as they are seen. They could make active changes in self-concept toward a more positive and realistic self-image. This experiment can be done in small or large groups, or one-to-one.

INSTRUCTIONS TO THE GROUP   Take a moment to stretch yourself up to standing position . . . meander to a place in the room where you'd like to begin. This experiment has three parts. It seems to work best to let your moving come "off the top," with no rehearsing. Any thing you do is just right.

I'd like you to move through the room *the way you see yourself moving through your life right now*. Let your body move like that until I ask you to pause.

(*Continue for 1–2 minutes, depending on degree of involvement.*)

Pause now and notice yourself in stillness. Notice how you feel inside right now, how your breath moves, where you feel most lively.

Now begin moving through the room *the way others see you moving through your life right now*. Others can be "them" or one other person or several different people in a row. Go ahead and begin moving. You may notice this part feels and looks different from the first. I'll signal you when to pause.

(Continue for 1–2 minutes, then pause.)

Great . . . now pause and focus inside yourself again. Notice any differences in the way you feel now.

Now let your body carry you through the room *the way you'd like to be moving through your life.* Go inside to the place that knows what you *really* like, and let your body move that way through the room. Go ahead.

(Continue for 2 minutes.)

Fine . . . let your moving take you back to your seat. Take out a piece of paper and write or draw something you learned about yourself.

VARIATION This experiment can be done in pairs, with one partner watching and giving feedback about what new things he or she sees in the other partner, or whether the way they see themselves is consistent with the way others see them or they want to be seen.

COMMENT Discussion of this experiment can be an opportunity for developing active listening skills. The emphasis is on reflection of the mover's activity rather than the watcher's opinions.

DISAPPEARING AND APPEARING

TO THE LEADER This experiment is designed to give participants sensory feedback about how much of their bodies they experience and what creates a sense of safety for them. Noticing the times and circumstances in which we tend to disappear can make us more aware, draw our attention to parts of us that are neglected, and give us more choice in our pace of moving through life.

INSTRUCTIONS TO THE GROUP   We're going to play an exaggeration game. How can you be here and *not* be here at the same time? You could go to sleep, or let your mind drift off into a memory of a fun time while your body stays in the room. For now, let's experiment with having different parts of us go away for a moment while the rest of us moves around as always.

Try on some different ways of hiding your mouth. You can cover it in lots of ways . . . hold it tightly, making a "stiff upper lip." . . . Play with different ways of making your mouth disappear. Let yourself exaggerate each part that you are hiding. Notice how making part of you disappear affects the rest of you. Good . . . now hide your stomach. Experiment with ways you can make your belly disappear . . . sucking it in . . . folding your arms across it. Find your own way of hiding your belly and make it really obvious. Great, now let's try hiding our hands. Our feet. Good.

Now let's go back to those parts we made disappear and see what happens when we breathe into them. Close your eyes and breathe warmth and space into your mouth and stomach and hands and feet. Take a moment to love them for helping you in all the ways they do, for being part of you.

COMMENT   Peripheral parts of the body (hands, feet, head) are easier to begin with in this experiment. As students become more familiar with hiding and reclaiming parts of themselves you may gradually add more central parts such as shoulders, chest, and hips. These areas tend to be more emotionally charged, that is, people become more anxious when they move the torso, the largest repository of unexpressed feeling, so pace your instructions to the comfort level of the students.

DRAW YOURSELF

TO THE LEADER   Self-image is like an iceberg: Most of our ideas and internal images of ourselves are under the surface of our awareness. This activity seems to draw out hidden aspects of the way we see ourselves, and can be useful in helping participants claim more of themselves.

You'll need fairly large paper and oil pastels or crayons. You'll also need space to draw and space to move.

INSTRUCTIONS TO THE GROUP   Come on over, get a sheet of paper, and pick one color crayon that especially appeals to you. Then take them back to your seat (*or to a place on the floor*).

Now, with your *eyes closed,* draw yourself. Don't open your eyes until you're finished. Don't cheat, you'll have more fun if you can surprise yourself.

(*Students will finish at different times, and will have different exclamations over their creations.*)

Okay, is everybody finished? What do you notice about

your drawing? Is it what you thought you were drawing? Does it look the way you see yourself, or different?

(*Take several minutes for sharing, emphasizing that there is no right or wrong way of doing this activity.*)

Now I'd like you to experiment with your drawing. Find a place in the room where you'd like to be, and look at your drawing in a special way. Notice the qualities and textures of your drawing. What pops out at you? Is it sharp, or fuzzy, or huge? Is some part of you tiny, or not where it is on your body? What is it like?

Look at your drawing until some part of it comes to your attention. Then let your body move that quality in the space around you until it feels a part of you. Then go back to your drawing again and notice something else, and then move your body in that way. Go back and forth several times.

(*Continue for 2–3 minutes.*)

Now let's do one more thing with our drawings. Pick up your paper and hold it in front of your chest. Walk through the room and greet other people you pass, being the character on your paper . . . meeting and greeting. Feel free to make sounds, too, but no words.

(*1–2 minutes.*)

Great. Let's go back to our seats.

COMMENT Small or large group discussion may uncover the messages students have incorporated about themselves: I'm too big, too tall; my feet are pigeon-toed; I have an ugly this or that. This experiment is designed to assist in owning all the parts of ourselves. Developing an accurate and positive self-image is the basis for enlivening encounters with the world and successful learning experiences.

MEETINGS AND GREETINGS

TO THE LEADER   This activity can be structured in pairs or by dividing the number of students and having them line up across from each other. (The second variation is described below.) It is designed to help develop satisfying ways of making contact with others, and to give students the opportunity to notice their preferences.

INSTRUCTIONS TO THE GROUP   Let's have half the students line up over on this side of the room and the other half over there. Face each other and get lined up opposite a partner.

Half of you are going to act and half of you are going to respond.

(Designate this division.)

Responders, here are your choices: When your partner comes to greet you, you can respond (1) positively and enthusiastically, or (2) negatively, as though you don't want contact, or (3) completely neutrally, stone-faced, with no visible response. I'd like you to decide each time *before* your partner approaches how you'll respond, although don't say how out loud. Any questions?

Now, Approachers, we're going to take several turns all going at once over to our partners and greeting them. We'll experiment with different ways of doing that and see what seems to work and how different approaches feel.

First, let's go over shyly. Approach your partner very hesitantly, maybe remembering some time when you felt a little uncomfortable, maybe excited but not sure, and exaggerate your movements. Okay, come back over to this side. Let's try being super loud and brash. Bowl over your partner. Okay, this time approach your partner at a different level, higher or lower in space.

VARIATIONS   Other ways of making contact include:

- with eyes closed
- backwards
- the way you *don't* like to be contacted

41

- sidling up
- looking everywhere but at your partner
- looking the way you do when you *have* to meet someone you like but you're not sure that person likes you
- pretending you're not really trying to meet the person even though you'd like to meet.

Pick a few each time, or choose variations that students suggest. Have the students switch roles after a few variations.

COMMENT   There will probably be lively comments as you move through this experiment. Time for talking can be integrated, and we recommend small group or partner sharing after this activity.

HORSE AND WAGON

TO THE LEADER   Sparking a sense of responsibility in students seems to be a critical and long-term goal of the educational process. If we understand our preferences more clearly and have the chance to try on different responses, we can increase our range of response-ability. This activity focuses on the choices we make about leading and following. Ideally, we want to be able to choose to follow when that's appropriate and lead when initiative is needed. Participants get to experience both modes in this activity.

INSTRUCTIONS TO THE GROUP   Find a partner, someone you don't know very well. Without speaking, decide who will be Partner One and who will be Partner Two. Good. Now, Partner Two, your job is to lead your partner around the room in as many ways as you can think of. It's okay to touch or not touch; see what works best. Partner One, I want you to really follow wherever your partner wants to take you. Notice whether you like or dislike different ways of being led. You can use sounds but no words. Okay, lead 'em out.

(*Do this for 2–3 minutes.*)

Now, Partner One, begin to let yourself not want to go along. Don't be so helpful. See if you can discover your favorite way of saying, no, I don't want to go.

(*Stop this section after 1–2 minutes while there's still plenty of energy, giving participants a brief taste of not going along.*)

Great . . . rest a moment and share with your partner what you enjoyed and what you didn't like.

Now let's switch roles. Partner One, you get to lead. Partner Two, you follow along. Be really cooperative until I signal you that it's time to not go along so easily.

COMMENT   Group discussion of this activity can uncover beliefs students have about appropriate role behavior and power issues. In the cognitive area, this activity can be used to illustrate sequences, as the title *horse and wagon* illustrates.

TO THE LEADER   Cultural and peer shaping of our behavior seems to blossom in the third and fourth grades, so that wondering how we'll be seen takes on great power. This activity is designed to filter and separate messages we've received about who we should be from the truth of our own experience. It is grounded in the recognition that we all have aspects of male and female within us, and works toward a satisfying balance of this fundamental polarity.

INSTRUCTIONS TO THE GROUP   Let's all move together for a while, exploring *opposites.* Our world has so many opposites: night and day, cold and hot, wet and dry, good and bad. Right now let's try on each word as though it were a piece of clothing. See how it fits you.

Let's start with *huge.* Let your body and movements be as big as you can.

(*Continue for 30 seconds.*)

Now let your body and your moving get *tiny,* as small as you can.

(*30 seconds.*)

Let your movements all be straight lines now, making your joints into angles.

(*30 seconds.*)

And now make curved lines in the space around you.

(*30 seconds.*)

Can your movements themselves be very loud?

(30 seconds.)

And now totally silent?

(30 seconds.)

Great, now move through the center of the room taking up lots of space, lots of elbow room.

(30 seconds.)

Now take up as little room as possible, making yourself into a beanpole.

(30 seconds.)

Now, each of you explore moving like a boy. How do boys act?

(Do this for 1 minute.)

Switch now, trying on moving as a girl does.

(1 minute.)

Notice for yourself whether your boy and girl movements were different or similar.

Pick a partner now, someone near you. Here's the rule of this game. When one of you is up toward the ceiling, the other must move down near the floor. It's as though you were two flags on two flagpoles, and if one is up the other must be down to be balanced. When either partner moves, the other must respond. If one moves down, the other must move up. All right, let's play one up, one down.

(Continue for 2–3 minutes.)

With the same partner, try a different experiment. When one of you advances, moves forward, the other must retreat, back up. Or if one of you retreats, the other must come forward.

(You might want to line up partners in the same direction if space is limited. Continue this for 2–3 minutes.)

Now take a few minutes to share discoveries with your partner.

VARIATION   Bring in pictures from different cultures that show the different ways men and women, boys and girls dress and interact. Have students try on these different modes in movement. You could also use paint dropcloths or pieces of material as costumes in this activity.

COMMENT   Other polarities can be added to the initial exploration: strong and weak, graceful and awkward, smart and dumb, balanced and off balance, cool and not cool. This exploration reveals that the experience of "I'm strong *and* sometimes I'm weak" leads toward more growth and integration; compare it, for example, with "I'm *either* real strong *or* a wipeout." The synthesis of experiential polarities is a major development task and useful tool.

5

Relaxation and sense awareness

CAT STRETCHES

TO THE LEADER   The cat is a great model for flexibility and comfort. Notice that each time the cat moves from a reclining state, he stretches the length of his body. That image of easy self-care is the basis for this experiment.

Stretching is one of the friendliest things we can do for ourselves, and it has many physical and emotional benefits. Helping students build stretching into their daily lives can prevent later degenerative changes and reinforce growing knowledge of their inner rhythms and their bodies' needs. It can be done next to desks, down on the floor, and in ways you invent.

INSTRUCTIONS TO THE GROUP   Close your eyes and let your mind remember the last time you saw a cat stretching itself. Let yourself experience that stretch as though the cat's body were your own. Imagine how your body would move and look, how that long S-curving would feel down your spine.

(*Hold for 10–15 seconds.*)

Good . . . now open your eyes and let your right arm stretch from top to toe the way a cat would stretch. Add your left arm. And rest.

Now find an open space and give your whole body a couple of feline flounces and cat stretches. Notice the way the stretch ripples through your body. Feel free to make yawning, sighing, and purring sounds with your stretches.

(*Hold for 30–60 seconds.*)

Now bring your stretched self back to your seat.

COMMENT   Once students have done cat stretches several times, they can be cued quite simply. Cat stretches provide quick work breaks. You might even declare a "cat stretch day," where everyone stretches *each* time she or he gets up from sitting or lying down.

BACK TAPPING

TO THE LEADER   This invigorating activity really wakes us up while relaxing the muscles we use to hold ourselves up all the time. It can be used as an interlude or prelude to another activity.

INSTRUCTIONS TO THE GROUP Find a partner and move to a place in the room where you'll have some space around you. Decide which of you has the tingly hands right now . . . great . . . you'll be the first tapper. Your partner will be the bender.

Bender, keep your knees loose as you slowly roll over from your head, leaning forward over your toes until you're hanging from your hips, back round, head loose and dropped. Good.

Now, Tapper, with loose wrists you're going to tap your hands along your partner's back, down the legs, up the back again, down and up the arms. Do not tap right on the backbone, but do tap gently on the back muscles. Ask your partner if the touch is just right, too hard, or too soft . . . let your touch be just perfect.

(*Do this for 2 minutes.*)

Now, Tapper, finish up, and Bender, roll back up to standing position *very* slowly, breathing easily and letting your head be the last part to come back up on top of your spine.

Good, now switch roles.

MAKING SPACE

TO THE LEADER   This experiment can be adapted to several settings, at desks or in open space in the room. It can be used as a stretch break or as an introduction to other spatial-awareness experiments.

INSTRUCTIONS TO THE GROUP   Breath makes space. Close your eyes and take a huge-to-bursting breath, and feel how big you are inside. Now let it out all at once and see if your body seems smaller. Take a breath and send it into your right arm. Let your right arm breathe out into the air around you; paint the air with your breath. Now take a breath into your left foot. Let the air out, sending it out through your foot, very slowly like a pinprick leak . . . ssssh . . . and let the leak move your foot through the air around you. Now send a breath into the middle of your back. How does the breath want to move you in space? Choose another part of you somewhere that needs a little space, and breathe a warm and cozy breath into it. Let the breath movement surprise you, let it move you through space.

TESTING THE WATER

TO THE LEADER Relaxing while moving and relaxing while following are both explored in this experiment, which comes from the martial art of T'ai Chi Ch'uan. Students might notice how they anticipate movement and where they tense their bodies in an unfamiliar situation. When this experiment is working well, participants report delicious sensations of floating, feeling a oneness with their partners, and deep relaxation. Use relaxation music as background (see the music reference list in the *References*).

INSTRUCTIONS TO THE GROUP Totally silently, find a partner and stand facing each other. Without talking about it, decide who will be Partner One and who will be Partner Two. Good.

Partner One, extend your favorite forearm in front of you, letting the rest of your body breathe out . . . hhaa.

Your arm is going to be the floor of the boat for your partner.

Partner Two, place your fingertips on your partner's forearm and rest them so they're heavier than feather light and lighter than an anchor. Find the most relaxed way of resting on your partner's arm.

Both partners, move your feet and legs in a rocking motion, one leg behind the other, until you feel settled and ready to move in any direction.

Partner Two, close your eyes and take a couple of deep breaths, releasing any ropes in your muscles with each out-breath. Partner One, begin to move your forearm in even, slow patterns through space, guiding your boat over gentle, rippling waves. You may want to close your eyes, too. Your job is to stay in contact with your partner and to guide him or her into the sea of relaxation. When you feel in touch with your partner, you can begin moving your feet as well, taking your boat through the room.

(Continue for 2–3 minutes. Encourage Partner One to make random patterns.)

Now slowly bring your forearm to a resting place, Partner One. Each of you take a few long, sighing breaths and stretch out your body for a moment, then switch roles.

COMMENT   It's valuable to have time after this experiment to let students share their experience, either verbally or by drawing or finger painting their sensations on paper. This has been a favorite relaxation for participants, and seems to be more fun each time it's done.

BACK BREATH

TO THE LEADER A warm room, carpet, and soft lights provide the best background for this experiment. It is designed to open up the back of the body to breathing, to provide a new way for students to be with each other, and to facilitate a sense of relaxation that might give students an opportunity to integrate information and experience. Participants occasionally fall asleep, so you might want to give them permission to do so.

INSTRUCTIONS TO THE GROUP Find a partner from the other side of the room. One of you, Partner One, lie down on your stomach on the floor. Take a few minutes to wiggle and stretch your body into a comfortable lying position where you can rest for several minutes. Partner Two, sit down cross-legged facing your partner's back on the right side, close enough that you can easily reach the middle of your partner's back.

Partner Two, watch your partner's breathing closely until you can see the place where there is the most rising and falling. Place your left hand gently but firmly in contact with that part of the back. Greet your partner through your touch. Watch and feel how far up the back her or his breath moves. Place your right hand *just beyond* the place where the breath moves, and rest it there.

Partner One, your only task is to *let* your breath move between the two hands. No pushing or oomphing, just allowing. Partner Two, as breath fills up the space between your hands, move one or the other again just beyond the moving place and wait until breath fills it up again. Take

54

your time, close your eyes from time to time to feel how the breath moves. You may eventually have your hands at both ends of your partner's back, or the breath may move up to the shoulder blades. How far doesn't matter.

(*Take 5–10 minutes depending on students' involvement.*)

Now, Partner Two, get ready to say goodbye with your hands. When you are ready, easily remove your hands and move away from your partner. Partner One, let your body begin to wake up again, opening your limbs and stretching out catlike as you gradually come back to the room.

After a few minutes, switch roles.

Solving problems

6

Solving problems

Learning to solve problems is an important goal in education, whether we are resolving temporary ownership of a soccer ball in elementary school or working out a marital disagreement in our fifties. Many of us wish we had learned effective problem-solving strategies early in life, so that we would not create as much conflict later on.

While problem solving is sometimes thought to be a rational and verbal process, there are ways of approaching problems with the whole body. Often the use of movement can provide the shift in perspective that is needed to clear up something people are stuck on.

On the following pages are experiments that can bring a refreshing whole-person perspective to problem resolution.

SEA TREES

TO THE LEADER   Often when a problem arises we go immediately to our heads to try to solve it. There are ways of solving problems that can use the whole of us.

If we are willing to see all of what is happening and to be all we are, then when we face a new situation or problem we can keep our balance and move from our center. Expanding to embrace the challenge is the focus of this experiment.

You might wish to have students remove their shoes when doing this activity.

INSTRUCTIONS TO THE GROUP   In puttylike slow motion, go to a place in the room where you can stand with space all around you. Shift your weight from side to side until you find the leg that feels most in touch with the floor. Let your weight settle down into your foot. Attach the bottom of your foot to the floor like a suction cup.

Keeping your other foot off the floor, let the rest of your body wave through the air as though you were surrounded by warm water that holds you up. Nibble, gobble, or slurp up whatever you need from the water/air around you. Especially reach from under your shoulders out through your fingers in all directions. Remember, your foot is stuck to the floor.

(*Continue for 2–3 minutes.*)

Now rest, and shake out your arms and legs for a moment. Try attaching the other leg to the floor, reaching and bringing in your catch. How does your body feel balancing on this side?

VARIATIONS   Here are two to read verbatim.

Think for a moment of a problem you have right now. How does this problem feel in your body? Let the problem attach your foot to the floor. Is it sticky or heavy or slippery? Let your whole body move around this problem, feeling it with all of you.

Choose a partner. Partner One, attach your foot like the stem of a flower, down into the ground. Let the rest of your body burst open toward the sun like the petals of a big flower. Remember that the other foot stays off the floor. Partner Two, whenever you lightly tap Partner One, the taps being raindrops, Partner One has to close up his or her petals to get out of the rain. After a moment, Partner Two, begin beaming your body at Partner One, swirling around like the warm sun. When you feel the sun, Partner One, begin to spin and spread your petals again. Do this several times, then switch roles.

COMMENT   Balance is connected to extension. Contracting away from a problem from fear or the belief we're not good enough keeps us from having access to all of our resources. Discussion of how we feel when we get smaller than we are, how we lose our balance when something new arises, and how to find it again could follow the experiment.

GETTING STUCK AND UNSTUCK

TO THE LEADER   Everybody gets stuck now and then. Life is not about trying to avoid being stuck; it's about how we get stuck and unstuck. Trying to avoid being stuck can *really* get us stuck. A workable measure of progress in life is how fast we get unstuck, how often we get stuck and unstuck. Being stuck is usually about something we need to learn or experience. This experiment explores some of the ways we get stuck and some possibilities for getting unstuck. If we learn to get unstuck in our bodies, we can generalize that knowledge to other areas.

INSTRUCTIONS TO THE GROUP   We're going to explore a place that we probably all know—getting *stuck*. Those times when you can't go this way *or* that, nothing seems right. Sound familiar? How do we get stuck, and how can we get unstuck? Let's experiment with this sticky situation.

First, try sticking a part of you to the floor. Really fasten it down, superglue it to the floor. Now explore all the ways you can move the rest of you that's not stuck.

(*Do this for 1 minute.*)

Now ask yourself what is needed to unglue that stuck

part? Try breathing into the stuck place, or imagining the glue dissolving into the floor, or inventing some other way. Now stick another part of you to the floor and see how you can move. Move as much as you can with that part *very* stuck.

(30–60 seconds.)

And then begin to unstick that part and let your body move all together . . . ahh, yes.

Now try sticking one part of you to another part of you, perhaps your elbow to your hand, or your foot to your thigh. You choose. Move around the room now with those parts stuck together, noticing how much you can move and how it feels.

(30–60 seconds.)

And now begin to unstick. Do you need to blow on the stuck place or rub it? What does your body need to unstick? Now try sticking one other part to another part of you and see how that changes your ability to move through the room.

(30–60 seconds.)

And again unstick, being aware of what this part of you needs. Good.

Let your whole body get stuck in one position. Try being stiff as a board or limp as a noodle. Can your body move when you're stuck like that? Try it . . . more and more until your body says let's try something else, and shifts.

(30–60 seconds.)

62

Is there another whole-body stuckness you do sometimes when you're mad or frustrated? Let your body get stuck in that feeling. No moving! When you feel *really* stuck, ask that stuck place directly: What do you need from me in order to get unstuck? Listen with your ears, and also let your breath open wide to make space for the answer.

(1–2 minutes.)

When you get unstuck let your body continue moving for a while, enjoying the freedom.

We can get stuck in an idea about ourselves, too, such as I'm not good enough or nobody likes me or I can't do that, it's too hard. Think for a moment of some idea you sometimes get stuck in. Let that idea mold your body like clay until you look and feel the same as your idea. When you're stuck, a little or a lot, take a moment to love yourself, hug yourself inside for having that idea sometimes. Then begin to think a different idea about yourself: I'm totally lovable; I *can* do it; I like myself. Watch the new idea begin to melt the old idea and remold the clay, making it softer.

(30–60 seconds.)

Enjoy your free moving, and then find your seat again.

VARIATIONS   In place of or in addition to the above, suggest that students get stuck in a particular movement pattern, a way of moving that's repeated such as limping or walking on tiptoe or leading with the head way out in front. Direct their attention to the changes that being stuck makes in how they notice other people, or their comfort and contact with themselves. Have them invent a new way of getting unstuck.

63

Another variation is to stick different parts of themselves to the chair or desk.

OBSTACLE COURSE

TO THE LEADER Problems often arise out of our placing obstacles between ourselves and what we want. In this experiment, participants construct their obstacles and learn to move through them. All types of environments are suitable for this one.

INSTRUCTIONS TO THE GROUP Sometimes to get where we want to go we need to go around and under and over. Let's play with making up an obstacle course. Each of you will make your own. First imagine something you want or somewhere you want to go . . . now imagine all kinds of things in the way . . . moats, walls, tunnels, dragons, canyons, winds, and storms.

Start somewhere in the room and move toward your goal, encountering each obstacle that gets in your way. Take your time to really do what needs to be done to clear up and get through each obstacle. This is your journey, so notice what you need to be successful with each thing you meet. Okay, let's go.

(*Continue for 5–8 minutes, depending on degree of involvement.*)

Let's share what happened.

THE BOX

TO THE LEADER This experiment can be used in a variety of ways, depending upon what's in the "box." It is structured here as a problem-solving activity; additional suggestions are listed afterwards. An open or semifurnished room is probably most suitable for this experiment. Music can provide a magical background; *Fantasia on a Theme by Thomas Tallis* by Vaughan Williams, *Mysterious Mountain* by Hovhaness, and any of Steve Reich's work are good journey music.

INSTRUCTIONS TO THE GROUP Think for a moment or two of some problem you've encountered recently that you'd like to solve. It could be a math or reading assignment, a difficult theme, or something that's occurred between you and a friend.

Now close your eyes and imagine a box somewhere in this room. See its shape and size . . . notice any decorations or colors on it. Inside this box is something that will help you solve your problem, something new.

Open your eyes and look at that place in your room, imaging your body there with your eyes open. Let your body begin to move toward the box. Are you excited to find out what's inside, or scared, or hesitant? As you move toward the box notice if anything gets in your way, or if you need to take a long path to get there. What is your own way of reaching your box?

As you approach your box, take time to explore its outside. How does the box feel to your hands? How big

65

is it? Let your imagination make it bigger than you are. Find out everything you can about it . . . how does it open? . . . does it have a padlock, a clasp, no lock? . . . how can you open the box?

When your box is opened, climb inside and shut the top, or leave a crack open so you can see out. Find out what is inside and take time to make it your own. Now find a way to bring what you've found back with you as you leave the box so that you can come back to the box for security and safety whenever you wish.

VARIATIONS   In the box is

- something you need to help you take the next step in your own journey
- a secret, something great about you that you didn't know
- something you've been missing
- limitless good feeling.

ROOM RUN

TO THE LEADER   There's more than one way to. . . . Flexibility is often the key to problem solving. Changing your perspective, seeing things another way, turning things upside down are expressions we use to describe the process of turning a problem over and examining new possibilities for solving it. This activity duplicates that process at the movement level. It can be a five-minute stretch break, an integral part of a new learning activity, or an extended experiment on its own.

INSTRUCTIONS TO THE GROUP   How do you usually get from one place to another? Use the whole length of the room and go across the way you usually do. Now we're going to experiment with many different ways of getting from here to there. I'll suggest a way each time you go across the room. Start by moving as slowly as you can

- without your feet touching the floor
- making circular patterns in space
- next to someone else
- without crossing anyone's path
- as quietly as you can
- leading with some part of you way out in front
- every way but front and straight ahead
- along the edges of the room
- backwards
- making straight lines in space with your body
- as fast as you can
- on one foot
- between you and a partner, using only two of your four feet and one of your four hands to touch the floor
- using neither your feet nor your hands
- via the most direct route
- the longest way you can imagine to get there

67

Solving problems

- eyes closed
- eyes open but looking over your shoulder.

COMMENT   Discussion can focus on the discoveries students make about the enormous variety of movement available when efficiency is not the most important consideration.

7

Building group cohesiveness

PASS THE ENERGY

TO THE LEADER   This experiment lets everyone be a magician and pull a shape out of the air. It can build a sense of group contact and develop resources for learning *how* to learn. It seems most effective when done with between ten and fifteen participants. If your group is larger, you might want to divide into two circles, in fishbowl style (one circle within the other, outer circle watching) or in two distinct circles with a leader for each group. Keep the action moving briskly until students get more familiar with the experiment.

INSTRUCTIONS TO THE GROUP   Let's sit in a circle. Take a moment to check that you can see everyone else. We're going to learn to create something out of nothing. First, rub your hands together very quickly until they're warm and tingly feeling. Now move them apart from and closer to each other several times, really paying attention to the space between them. The air may feel heavier, or as though you're pushing against something.

(*Take a moment to share short words and phrases describing this sensation.*)

Okay, now rub your hands together again and build up another tingle.

(*Choose a student to demonstrate the activity.*)

Form that space between your hands into a ball, any size, any weight. Let us see from your movements what it's like. Good, now throw it to someone. See if you catch the same ball that was thrown. Good, now change its size and throw it to someone else . . . catch it and change its weight, and throw it.

(*Continue for 3–4 more throws.*)

Now toss the ball up into the air and stick it to the ceiling.

I'm going to use the space between my hands to make a shape. See if you can tell what it is. I'll pass it now to _____ (*person on right or left*). When you receive the shape just as it is, then you can remold it, adding energy or taking it away as you like. See what the energy wants to do with your hands. Pass it when it's done, on around the circle.

COMMENT Your focus and attention as leader can spark the students' enthusiasm and encourage development of

71

coordination and group rapport. Sometimes two or more trips around the circle may seem appropriate if new ideas and forms arise. The last person can "dispose" of the energy or find a way to include the whole group in giving it away.

GET MY ATTENTION

TO THE LEADER Attention is an important aspect of our communication with each other. Discovering what works and what doesn't in establishing contact with another person is a crucial building block in effective interaction styles. This experiment can give participants feedback about their style of communicating. It also can provide a safe outlet for what psychologists call resistance and what you may call orneryness.

INSTRUCTIONS TO THE GROUP Find a partner and stand next to her or him. Decide who will be Partner One and who will be Partner Two. In this experiment Partner One is going to try to get Partner Two's attention. You'll know that's happened when Partner One *looks* at you, makes eye contact. Partner Two, you can wait a while to make eye contact if you wish. Any questions? Okay, go!

> (*Continue for 2–3 minutes. Students might want to know what behaviors are permissible or off limits such as making loud noises, touching, etc. From your knowledge of your students, decide what boundaries will provide safety and also let your students experiment spontaneously.*)

Now take some time to talk with your partner about what you liked and didn't like, what seemed to work. You may notice that some ways of getting attention were familiar and some ways that other people were using were unfamiliar.

Now switch roles. Partner Two, you try to get Partner One's attention, and Partner One, you withhold eye contact for a while. Experiment with different strategies.

(2–3 minutes.)

Now take some time to talk with your partner about your experience.

COMMENT   Group discussion following this experiment can be especially valuable to clarify effective, appropriate channels for giving and receiving attention, and can help to prevent later communication problems from developing. Helping students identify their preferences for being approached can assist them to be clearer in their interactions no matter what the content.

SWITCH

TO THE LEADER   This experiment explores an active form of mirroring or reflecting movement. It can sharpen participants' perceptual motor skills while they learn more about nonverbal communication. This experiment requires an open space. It involves more spontaneous participation than other group activities, so might best be introduced after students have done some group-process experiments.

Building group cohesiveness

Music with a strong underlying rhythm would be useful here, such as square dance music, a popular rock song, African drumming, and so on.

INSTRUCTIONS TO THE GROUP   Let's move into a circle. Follow me for a moment and let's stretch our arms up and wide. Does anyone else have a way of stretching?

(Take turns following 1–3 other stretches.)

We're going to take turns switching movements. We'll use the center of the circle to move. Two at a time, move into the center of the circle any way you like. Make a movement you *repeat* and do it a few times while you watch your partner. When I say switch, trade movements and leave the center of the circle moving the way your partner did. So you'll go in your way and come out a different way.

(Orchestrate the action, the timing or pacing of this activity, by picking the two movers and saying switch. Give everyone a chance to play. If there is time, let some students have another turn.)

VARIATIONS   Move into the center

- in the silliest way you can imagine
- the way you do when you are "putting your best foot forward"
- shyly and hesitantly
- as your favorite animal would.

Exploring the
transpersonal realm

As teachers, we want our students to appreciate the full range of human experience. The transpersonal realm, although it goes far beyond what is usually considered traditional in education, is something for which most of us feel a deep yearning. We want to experience completion, wholeness, union, divinity, to feel what is sacred within us and around us. Here are several activities designed to take us beyond the limited realm of the ego into the boundless dimension of the transpersonal.

EXPANSIVE IMAGING

TO THE LEADER Being more ourselves, moving beyond our conceptions of who we are, can occur in many ways. The use of active imaging is a vital and immediate method for participants to find their relationship to the powerful forces in the world. These activities each have a central image that participants are invited to assimilate. Relaxation, journey, or emotionally evocative music is recommended (see *References*).

INSTRUCTIONS TO THE GROUP Wherever you are in the room right now, close your eyes and pretend that the sun is not out there in the sky but inside you and glowing very brightly right in the middle of your belly. Let its warmth and light fill you all up and then spill out in all directions, lighting up the room. Keep shining as you open your eyes and let the sun's rays dance through you. You are the sun! Let your warmth flow out into the room . . . send your light toward someone else now, beaming and dancing over that person . . . and now let your sun body shine on someone else, give that person all your light, and notice there's still more.

(You might have students direct their light to someone who's not present, a friend, relative, or classmate.)

Next, choose a partner and decide who will be the tree and who will be the wind. Wind, you have many possibilities within you. You can puff and hiss or you can flutter and billow, as you choose. Tree, your roots go deep into the earth. You can be tall and massive or slender and supple, as you choose. Wind and tree, move together, noticing how you affect each other.

(Continue for 2–3 minutes.)

Wind, let yourself become more solid inside until you become a tree. Tree, let the wind's breath dissolve your "treeness" until you have no solidity and you become the wind. And now, Tree and Wind, move together.

Next, let your body stretch out through your toes and fingertips, getting larger and thinner until you feel you could float away. And you *can,* imagining you're a kite, a beautiful bright kite in the air. And you can go wherever you want on the wind, no string holds you. Fly where you want to go!

Gurgling . . . bubbling . . . splashing . . . now be in a stream of water. Let it carry you flashing over rocks, around bends . . . let the water in and through you . . . until you *are* the stream rolling along. Where are you going? What do you see along your shores?

(*You can take the stream into the river and then the ocean if you wish.*)

JOURNEY

TO THE LEADER   This activity is designed both to open new internal resources for learning and to affirm the wholeness in each of us. The journey is an archetypal process with many possible levels of meaning: Our lives are a journey, school is certainly a journey, self-discovery is perhaps the most awesome journey. This journey leads to the inner teacher, what we perhaps have called conscience or the small inner voice. The inner teacher can provide surprising new resources and perspectives and help build a sense of self-support, responsibility, and connection with transpersonal realms of experience. The music selection for the journey is especially important for the tone it sets. The music list in the *References* has several selections for journeys. You won't necessarily need an open space but you will need sufficient moving room and a soft floor; the opening section can be done in chairs if the floor is not carpeted.

INSTRUCTIONS TO THE GROUP   Find a comfortable place in the room and lie down on the floor. Stretch out, yawn and sigh, find the muscles that need to roam, and wiggle and squirm them. Close your eyes . . . notice your body against the floor, where it feels hard and where you feel soft into the floor. Now release your muscles into the floor, let the floor hold you easily, gently. Take a large balloon breath in and let it out through your mouth . . . again, big breath in, out all at once. Good, now imagine a big pink scarf floating across your body up from your toes to your head. As it touches each part of you it relaxes and warms you . . . toes . . . ankles . . . legs . . . knees . . . thighs . . . hips . . . belly . . . chest . . . shoulders . . . neck . . . face . . . all warmed and comfortable. Let the scarf pass over you once more to release any other tense parts so your body is heavy and feeling good.

Inside your mind, imagine a natural place where you'd like to be. It could be a tall green meadow, the seashore, or up in the mountains. Notice where you want to be . . . see the colors and feel the warmth of the sun on

79

your face . . . any smells of flowers or water and the feel of the breeze on your skin.

You're going on a search in this place you've found in your mind . . . let the scene in your mind fill this room so that when you gently open your eyes you can bring your relaxation and your place here. Take some time.

Now, let your body explore this nature scene in this room, really enjoying it. You're looking for something and you don't quite know what it is . . . searching in this place.

(*Take 1–2 minutes.*)

Let your search take you down, underground. What do you find there?

(*1–2 minutes.*)

Let your search take you uphill, climbing.

(*1–2 minutes.*)

You're looking for someone. Somewhere on the mountain you'll find the home of the person you're looking for. When you find it ask that person whatever you most want to know right now. The person may answer you in a surprising way. Be aware all around you. Take time to be with this person.

(*Continue for 1–2 minutes.*)

If you like, you can choose another time and place to meet with this person again, but for now, say goodbye and begin moving down the mountain to the place you started your journey. Notice anything new you didn't experience before.

(1–2 minutes.)

And let yourself sink back into the floor, enjoying in your mind and body your adventure . . . then stretch easily and wake up again, refreshed and recharged.

COMMENT Drawing or writing about this activity afterwards helps integrate the experience. Fantasy movement is a skill that becomes easier and richer with repetition. Feel free to vary the locations and questions of this journey as your class becomes skilled at moving while relaxed.

DREAM HOUSE

TO THE LEADER The house is one traditional metaphor for the personality. All the rooms in the house are aspects of the personality, some familiar, like the living room, and some dusty and dark, like the attic and the basement. In this activity, participants create their houses and then explore them. Actual dreams of houses and buildings can also be used for exploration. Drawing the houses afterwards can be useful. A room with the available open space is most suitable.

INSTRUCTIONS TO THE GROUP Take a moment to stretch your body as you're seated, getting comfortable. Close your eyes and let your mind create a path leading over a hill. In the distance is a house. Come up to the house and move around it, exploring it from the outside. When you're ready, find a way inside the house. As you begin to explore the house, let your body move through *this* room, changing it into your special house. Explore all the rooms and whatever is in them . . . upstairs and downstairs . . . hidden rooms . . . locked doors . . . whatever you find.

(Explore for 2–3 minutes.)

Then come back to your seat and draw something you discovered in your house or something you especially liked.

VARIATIONS   You can lead students through the relaxation section of the previous exercise, "Journey," or all of "Fluffing" in Chapter 3 before starting this activity. You can also instruct students to "become" their houses, letting their bodies move the qualities they discover.

MOVIE DIRECTOR

TO THE LEADER   This activity is based on the students' dreams, and gives a group of students the opportunity to enter another person's inner life. The instructions for this experiment are rather general, as each dream is different. After some group sharing of dreams, ask one student to repeat her or his dream in the present tense. Then, as director, have the students assign parts to each other, *showing* them how to move and where to be in the room. Every aspect of the dream can be given as a role, even objects and trees, the sky, and the feeling of the dream. When everyone has a part, the director assigns her- or himself a part and the class reruns the dream.

VARIATIONS   The director takes different parts. If you have an intuition about a part that would be valuable to explore, suggest that.

Another student takes the part of director after a run-through and gives another active interpretation.

FAIRY TALES

TO THE LEADER   Fairy tales are some of the richest sources of drama, life scripts, transcendence, and learning life's lessons that we have. There are many different ways to explore fairy tales. We'll suggest a few. For musical accompaniment, consult the *References* for ethnic or group interaction selections.

INSTRUCTIONS TO THE GROUP   What are your favorite fairy tale characters? Let's make a sample list together:

Prince Charming	Wicked Stepmother
the Princess	Rapunzel
the frog	Aladdin
Ugly Duckling	Little Red Riding Hood
Snow White	Sleeping Beauty
Rumpelstiltskin	Pied Piper
Hansel and Gretel	

As a group, let's pretend to be some of these people. Let yourself stand and walk the way they would, greeting people you pass in character.

(*Call out various characters.*)

Let's pick one tale and act it out. First I'll read it through and you sit with your eyes closed and let yourself travel back to that time and place, seeing and hearing what it must have been like.

Now I'll put on some music and let you move through the tale yourself, encountering all the events and people as the tale unfolds. Let yourself become larger than life as you transform your world.

VARIATIONS   Assign roles from a fairy tale to different students, and have other students become other aspects of the environment, such as the castle tower or the moat or the briar patch.

Use costumes when moving through the tale.

Have students make up their own fairy tales, moving, drawing, and writing them.

Exploring time

The qualities of time, space, and weight are the abc's of the moving curriculum. Because they are fundamental, concrete building blocks of all movement structure, we have devoted a chapter to each. Our attitudes about time, space, and weight exert tremendous influence on our daily experience. A clear experiential understanding of these influences can provide a sound base for healthy development and more complex abstraction.

We asked a class to consider leaving their watches at home for a week, and the response was horrified confusion: How will I know what time it is? I have a tight schedule as it is! As adults, most of us are run by our time demands and stress our bodies constantly in the attempt to catch up. As children, most of us experienced many "hurry up" messages. A child's sense of wonder and exploration often doesn't match the demands of family life. It's all too easy to be pulled away from our innate connection with the flow of natural time as we become socialized. Our culture's obsession with time might be a great contributor to the rate of stress-related illness most of us encounter. The experiments in this chapter and elsewhere encourage a broader perspective on and experience of time. One of the kindest gifts we can give ourselves is to slow down.

Our sense of time is related to the style in which we make decisions, the ease or urgency of our course through daily life. The sense of being in harmony with the flow of life is confluent with our innermost rhythms. This chapter's activities are designed to increase participants' awareness of choices about time and to experience a renewed harmony between internal time and external events. This chapter treats time as a quality, not a quantity.

STRETCHING SPACE

TO THE LEADER   In this experiment, both internal choice and awareness of others are explored. This experiment requires open space.

INSTRUCTIONS TO THE GROUP   For the duration of this game you'll *keep moving*. You can go as fast or as slowly as you wish, that's your choice. Move closer to someone in the room until you're as close as you want to be, then begin moving away until you're as far from people as you want to be. Then move closer, then farther away. Okay, everyone begin.

(*Move for 1–2 minutes.*)

Move in from the side and from the back. How does changing your speed change your wanting to be closer or farther away? Change the level of your moving, go higher or lower. Where are you moving from in your body? And now rest, noticing how you feel, what you see and hear in the room.

COMMENT Group or paired discussion can relate this experiment to communication issues, how we decide what we want and where we want to go in our lives, and our choices to respect others' spatial needs.

WHAT TIME AM I?

TO THE LEADER Our sense of time and rhythm has its roots in our experience of the seasons and tides, the cycles of the sun and moon, as well as our internal, biological cycles. A sense of and grounding in our deepest rhythms seems essential to a sense of self, of autonomous identity. We know that most dis-eases are accompanied by dysynchrony, lack of synchrony between internal experience and self-evaluation and perception. By exploring and knowing ourselves as the source of time, rather than being run by it through clocks and rigid schedules, we may increase our sense of harmonious relationship within and without.

INSTRUCTIONS TO THE GROUP How many kinds of *slow* are there? Mill about the room, going from one place to another, as though you were in a movie and the camera speed got slower and slower. Now move across the floor pretending you're on your way somewhere you *have* to go, and feel that kind of slowness. Imagine you are dropped into a vat of sticky caramel and try to get out. Let your body stretch and yawn as though it were Saturday morning and a whole day that's all yours were in front of you. See if you can find another kind of slow moving particularly your own.

How many kinds of *fast* are there? Let that movie camera speed up now . . . and pause . . . and move through the room as though you were late and needed to get somewhere *right now*. Move being the wind blowing through the trees . . . fly like the hummingbird, whose wings move it at 90 mph! . . . or a blip in an electronic game. Go through the room as though you were on your way to meet your best friend. Do you have another way of being fast? Try it now.

What's your own favorite pace, the speed that makes you feel best? Move at that speed and notice other people as you move through the room. Can you keep your favorite speed if someone else is moving at a different pace? And now let your favorite speed lead you back to your seat.

SPIRALLING TIME

TO THE LEADER This experiment can be used with any repetitive movement, so the students can be in their seats or moving through an open space. Restless points in the day are especially good times to use this experiment. The example will use walking, but you can also use arm swinging, stretching, any arm or foot patterns such as shuffling, and so on. It is useful to pick a movement you see students repeating a lot, as different mannerisms make their way through the class.

INSTRUCTIONS TO THE GROUP   Begin walking in a circle at your own most familiar speed. It may be faster or slower than those around you. Now begin walking a little faster, and faster . . . more quickly . . . gradually moving as fast as you can . . . and then just begin to slow down . . . a little slower . . . even more . . . and slower and slower, still walking, until your body just winds down and stops. Rest there a moment. Now smoothly and evenly begin your walk, as though you were a robot just switched on and a little bit slow to start. Gradually speed up, faster and faster, until you're zooming along, and then slow down, slower and slower, and stop.

OCEAN EVOLUTION

TO THE LEADER   This experiment explores an individual sense of time in an imaginary environment. It can be a deeply renewing and refreshing interval. You can determine the length of the experiment by your choice of music (see the list in the *References*) and your pacing of the instructions. You'll need softer lights and a soft surface with open space.

INSTRUCTIONS TO THE GROUP   Meander through the room as a stream wanders over the ground . . . flow along with no need to go anywhere in particular . . . let the streaming grow larger inside you until you flow along in a river . . . water everywhere . . . moving toward the ocean. Feel yourself glide out into endless, soft water . . . sinking and finding that you can breathe underwater . . . drifting down to the floor of the ocean. Close your eyes and let go into the currents of the water gently tugging and shifting you along the bottom. What ocean creature would you like to be? . . . a minnow . . . a whale . . . a jellyfish bobbing . . . you choose. Become your creature and find the way you move in water. Let your creature change whenever you want. You can swim up through the water, leap out of the water, or stay along the floor . . . you're completely held and rocked by the water.

(*Continue for 2–5 minutes.*)

Now begin to float or swim up toward the shore. When you come to land, let your ocean-creature skin fall away, leaving you brand new inside as you climb on land and rest for a moment. Then open your eyes gently, stretch out, and come back to the room.

Exploring space

When we move, we occupy and define the space around us. Our use of space signifies our interest in our environment. Some people charge through space, going after what they want. Others shrink away from space, asking permission with their bodies to be present. This chapter explores some of our attitudes about space and what communication has to do with the way we form our bodies in interactions. We each have preferences for closeness and distance from others, and habits we've developed in shaping our living space.

Our primary living space is the area within arm's reach around our bodies, known sometimes as one's personal space or kinesphere. Personal space is like a rainbow stretching out from our internal experience of space, from the freedom or restriction of breath, feelings, and muscles.

This rainbow reflects the hues and tones of our insides as it communicates our sense of belonging in the world. The ability to understand and manipulate spatial relationships is a recognized aspect of intelligence. The more we interact with space, the more our learning matrix expands.

Interactional space relationships have been the focus of many research studies, and much is known about the role of spatial relationships in communication patterns. Issues of control, dominance, privacy, courtship, effective communication, and so on are familiar to anyone who has ridden in an elevator, attended a committee meeting, or walked a busy street. Our attitudes about space are powerful factors in our daily experiences and can be explored and clarified in movement experiments.

These activities touch on some fundamental aspects of spatial exploration. They can be used individually or in combination with activities from other chapters. Spatial awareness also appears in many of the experiments in other chapters (see the *Index*).

SPACE CAPSULE

TO THE LEADER   This experiment focuses on what we call personal space. Sensing and claiming our individual space can develop greater self-assurance and confidence in interactions, as well as circumvent the cause of many discipline problems.

INSTRUCTIONS TO THE GROUP   How many of you have seen the space capsules the astronauts used?

Exploring space

(*Conduct a brief discussion.*)

You live in a capsule all the time, and you take it with you wherever you go. You and I can't *see* it, but we do see what you do in your capsule, whether you like it, whether you use all of it or only some dusty, dark corners. That capsule is your space capsule, and it's all yours. You decide how big it is and how it feels. And you can remodel any time.

Find a place to stand in this room with no furniture close by and no other students within arm's reach. Let your feet be the launching pad of your capsule. They won't move around. Close your eyes and take a few deep breaths. Notice where the breath travels in your body. Let your eyes remain closed throughout this experiment. Use your arms and hands, your knees, the back of your head, different parts of you to reach out around you and explore your space capsule. How high is it . . . how wide? Where is the place you most like to be? Do you feel any closets with closed doors . . . any places that seem colder or smaller? Does your capsule have colors? What kind of surface does your capsule have, smooth or bumpy, thin or thick? Can you see through it with your inner eye? Get to know your own space capsule.

Slowly open your eyes and begin to walk about this room. Does your space bubble come with you? Does it change shape? How? What happens when you sit down?

COMMENT   Having the students draw or paint their space capsules can be valuable after this experiment.

SPACE TAG

TO THE LEADER   This experiment encourages development of spatial awareness, both personal and interpersonal. You'll need a large open space in which to explore, possibly outdoors or in the gym.

INSTRUCTIONS TO THE GROUP   Find your own open place. Take a moment to reach all around you in as many directions as you can without moving your feet. This is your own space bubble. Feel how large it is! And get acquainted with parts of it you haven't visited in a while. This game is done in slow motion, as though your space bubble were floating on a light breeze. Your aim is to tag other people's bubbles without letting yours be touched. Okay, float. If you get tagged, let all the air out of your space bubble the way air leaves a balloon with a leak. Let it take you zigzagging through space. If you get deflated, take a moment to remake your space bubble and rejoin the game.

COMMENT   You may want an umpire to confirm tagging when you first play this game. Later, students will probably discover that getting tagged is just as much fun as tagging.

SAFE SPACE

TO THE LEADER   Recent social psychology research indicates a strong connection between a sense of safety and the level of exploration attempted. We know that we need to move in order to perceive and learn, but we often forget that curiosity and wonder grow most freely from a firm base of comfort. In this activity, participants re-create the necessary aspects of their individual safety needs. A rich musical background can add to the quality of this activity. As this experiment is more unstructured and student-generated, you may wish to introduce it in conjunction with another activity or after students experience more structured activities.

INSTRUCTIONS TO THE GROUP   Your well-being is important, that sense of feeling at home in your body, welcome as you are. Let's take some time to actually look at and explore what we need to feel comfortable and safe as we move through the day.

Let your feet take you slowly through the room, no place to go, just sending out your antennae to sense how different parts of the room feel to you. How much space do you like around you? Where does your body like to be in the room? Let your body tell you whether you'd like to be standing, sitting, or lying down. Use anything in the room that adds to your sense of ease and comfort. If you want to be under something, great; if you like to be curled up, great.

(Wait for 2–3 minutes until students seem settled in a place in the room.)

Now let your internal motor slow *way* down until you can almost hear your heart beating. Be aware of whether you like to have your eyes open or closed. Take all the time you need to spread out inside yourself and find the way of moving that feels most delicious to you. Let your body be held by the space all around you. Try on different things . . . swaying, rocking, stretching . . . until you click into your own most comfortable way of moving.

(2–5 minutes.)

Wonderful . . . almost like taking a long nap. Now let your body begin to stretch and wake up and come back to the room. You can bring as much of your sense of comfort with you as you like.

COMMENT   When this activity is more familiar, it can be condensed as a stretch break and reminder to value ourselves.

SOUNDING

TO THE LEADER   This partner activity focuses on the interplay between internal space and what we perceive. Participants are usually amazed to find the consistency between hearing, seeing, and moving.

INSTRUCTIONS TO THE GROUP   Stand facing a partner and decide who'll be Partner One and Partner Two. Partner One, you'll be the first sounder. Partner Two, you'll listen with all of you, and you'll have your eyes closed at first.

Here's the game. Partner One, you take a full, deep breath, and make a sound and a movement together, a sound and movement that fit each other, big or small, your choice. Partner Two's eyes will be closed while you do this. Then Partner Two, open your eyes and see if you can repeat your partner's movement as you make the same sound.

Then switch parts. Partner Two, you be the sounder, and Partner One, you be the listener. Switch back and forth, taking turns with different sounds and movements. You might notice that it gets easier as you let your whole body be a big eardrum.

Any questions? Okay, let's sound.

(*Continue for 3–5 minutes.*)

Exploring weight

We are concerned in this chapter with our relationship with weight, the way we experience the relative solidity of our bodies. A weighty argument, a feather-light touch, a sense of being off-center, all can remind us of the basic nature of the sense of weight. Gravity is the most fundamental aspect of weight that we all deal with so constantly that we're generally not aware of the ever-present pull of the earth. Awareness of this relationship can increase our overall responsiveness to the ups and downs of life. If we can get behind our weight, we can have real impact. Conversely, if we give up, our weight tends to give in, to pool into a blob, and we are less effective in our interactions with others. Sensitivity in communication depends largely on our fluidity along the weight continuum from the delicate suggestion to the demand.

The experience of being centered is grounded in our sense of weight. Activating the movement potential of the pelvis awakens a true power and groundedness that allows us both to sink into the support of the earth and to reach out to others. Weight is related to support, both self-support and the capacity to encompass another's needs.

The activities in this chapter introduce different facets of weight. As with time and space, weight factors are integral parts of other experiments. Consult the *Index* for these listings.

SAILOR WALKING

TO THE LEADER   This experiment focuses on the moving center of the body. It is particularly designed to help ground and relax students in a way that can be generalized to other activities.

INSTRUCTIONS TO THE GROUP   Some sea movies show sailors down on the dock dancing to a sea chantey. They hold their arms in a certain way that I'd like you to try. Hold one forearm over your lower belly and bend the other behind you over the small of your back. Yo ho ho and away we go! Feel your breath move your hands in and out. Rest them gently against you as you begin walking a few steps forward, a few back. Let your body move from your belly and pelvis. Do you walk differently when you move back-wards? Try moving in a circle or sideways and notice any changes in your sailor ways. Hold your breath a moment as you walk. Does that change your sense of being low in your torso? Now take some breaths deep into your lower back. Does your hand move? Now for a moment lower your arms and see if you can keep the same sense of moving from your center, gliding along easily and smoothly. Great!

BUILDING BLOCKS

TO THE LEADER   We can use our weight in many different ways. Finding ways of supporting others and receiving support is one of the most satisfying. A carpeted, open space is most suitable for this experiment. It's helpful to emphasize the trust-building possibilities of this experiment to assist students in taking care of each other.

INSTRUCTIONS TO THE GROUP   Find a partner close to your own size. We're going to experiment with using our weight to build different shapes and structures with each other. First, put your hands against your partner's as though you were going to push. Let your bodies begin to lean toward each other, bending from the ankle, until you make an A shape. Notice that each of you needs to cooperate to make it work. Now slowly come back to standing upright, sup-porting your own weight. Try that once more. Now stand beside your partner and find a way of leaning shoulders against each other so that you are both supporting each other. And gently come back up. Now take some time to experiment with taking turns holding most or all of each other's weight. Feel free to try something interesting you see another pair doing.

Let your partner know what you want if you need more support or a different shape. Take a few minutes to talk to your partner. What felt easy and comfortable? Was any position scary? Did you feel you could hold your partner's weight? What did you like and not like?

VARIATIONS Try some other positions . . . back leaning; one partner in horseback position, the other astride; both sitting down leaning on their elbows with their feet touching, legs up in air.

BACKING

TO THE LEADER I'll back you up. Who's backing this deal? Do you have a back-up? These are some common phrases we use to talk about the experience of supporting each other. We tend to be so goal oriented, forward rushing, that our backs are largely unfamiliar territory. Self-support and support from others can flow from the back as well.

You'll need an open space in the room for this experiment.

INSTRUCTIONS TO THE GROUP Begin to walk backwards through the room, no peeking over your shoulders. Move slowly enough that you can begin to put eyes on the back of your head *and* on your back. Spread your back and arms out wide as you back through the room, seeing in a new way. Find the open path in the room. Notice how differently your body feels moving this way, whether your legs are sure or trembly, your breath full or fluttery.

Now look through your back for another person. Hook up with the back of a partner. Play with breathing through your back into your partner's back. Shift your weight and feel your partner's response. Does all of your back touch your partner's? What happens if you bend and stretch your back? Now say goodbye through your back and move to another partner. Explore backing with your new partner.

(*Decide how many partner changes you want.*)

Now see if you can back to your seats in the room.

POWER SHARING

TO THE LEADER   Experiencing our weight in different ways affects our sense of power or powerlessness, our ability to have impact, to be seen *and* heard. This experiment is a kind of movement brainstorming designed to give everyone a feeling of inner power and well-being. It is most suitable in an open space, although after first being introduced it can be adapted to the seating arrangements in which students spend most of their time.

INSTRUCTIONS TO THE GROUP   Let's form a standing circle. Let your arms be rotating airplane props for a moment and check to see if you have enough clean air space. Step back a step or so if you need more room.

Sometimes when we explore a theme, we get together and share ideas "off the top of our heads," what we call brainstorming. We're going to brainstorm in movement, shape our bodies into sculptures.

Close your eyes a moment, and scan back to the last time something happened and you felt helpless to do anything about it . . . something didn't go right. How did you feel inside and what did you want to say? Now open your eyes and let your body take on the shape that matches that feeling. Let's look around the circle and notice how many different ways our bodies can show powerlessness. Find someone else's way of expressing and try it on with your body. Notice if you feel differently holding your body another way. And try on one more person's stance. Are there any sounds that go with your way of standing? . . . sighs . . . squeaks . . . groans? Make a sound that goes with your position. Good, now bounce up and down just a moment and shake off that feeling and experience, clear your body. Ahh . . . good.

Close your eyes again and remember the last time you felt really big and strong and important, a time when you made an important decision. With your eyes closed let your body remember your way of standing, your sense of how much space you took up, your feeling of your feet against the floor. Take on that position of feeling powerful.

Then open your eyes and notice the difference in how everyone is standing. After a moment, again try on another person's sculpture . . . and one more person's position. What do these powerful positions have in common? Are they all different or was there something you noticed that was present in all the positions you tried on?

(*Take a few minutes to share, and have the whole group try on someone's powerful stance if possible.*)

Great, now close your eyes once more and imagine into the future. You have a *delicious* warm feeling of well-being because you have everything you need inside to feel just right. Notice what you need to have that sense of well-being, and notice how good it feels. When you are ready gently open your eyes and move through the room letting your sense of well-being carry you.

(*Continue for 1–2 minutes.*)

Great! Now let your steps take you back to your seat.

VARIATIONS For remembering experiences of empowerment: remember a time when

- you had a big problem to solve and finally got it
- you first rode your bike, or learned to do something really hard physically
- the whole day was so easy and fun and filled with adventure.

Translating learning objectives into movement

One major objective of this book is to introduce the possibility of learning while moving. In this section we want to address the question, How do I translate my own learning objectives into movement? There are a few key assumptions and attitudes and a few simple guidelines that facilitate this translation process.

An assumption central to this book is the consistency and congruency of human beings at different levels of experience. The moving person is a system of interrelated parts. The way we think we look affects the way we move. Our beliefs about the way the world works shape our bodies over time and determine how much freedom of choice we use. Self-image, body image is an influential dynamic in our ability to learn *how* to learn. For example, teaching a group of youngsters the fundamentals of math requires far less effort than teaching a group of older children fractions when they have adopted an "I can't do math" or "I'm not good in math" attitude. So, since the person is a bodymind system, altering movement patterns will alter the system and will affect cognitive, emotional, and social aspects of the same theme.

The translation process is built around identifying the theme you wish to explore, the curriculum objective, the area of the topic you wish to emphasize. Words or phrases can be themes: *character, the action in this story, mysteries, ravine, maps*. Processes can also be themes: *tracing the outline, finding the map coordinates, making a simple sentence, dividing in half*. Recognizing that we experience through our bodies, even what we read and think, can assist us in opening up the movement possibilities of most situations, locating the central theme.

When developing your own movement activities, these sequential directions seem to give clear guidelines with room to maneuver:

1. Start with moving body parts and gradually include more of the body. Giving the direction, "Begin to move your hands in round lines through space," is likely to be more effective than saying, "Let's move our bodies in round ways."

2. Involve the periphery of the body before moving into torso integration in the sequence. Hands, feet, and heads are more social and generally well-liked parts of people's bodies. People will generally much more readily move these peripheral parts than the

trunk of the body, which is more vulnerable, contains most emotional expression, and might be more guarded.

3. Feel confident in structuring your initial directions, moving gradually toward less structure as the class gets familiar with the activity. Specific, concrete directions at the beginning provide safety and boundaries within which the students can experiment. For example, the initial direction, "Use just your left arm to move away from your side and then back toward it," would be more effective than saying, "Move some part so you feel you're making space."

4. Contrasting and exaggerating are wonderful tools that you can feel free to repeat and repeat. Exaggerating a theme with the body can bring its qualities into relief. For example, if our theme were *sizes,* the qualities of big, bigger, and biggest could be translated easily into exaggerated body movement. Contrasting is doing the opposite, and is very useful in exploring the many polarities of our lives: day and night, hot and cold, up and down, huge and tiny, before and behind, and so on. Learning difficulties can often be solved by noticing which polarity the student is expressing and encouraging him or her to do the opposite. For example, moving while saying I don't know! in as many ways as the student can imagine can be alternated with I know! statements and gestures.

When beginning to use these guidelines, remember that you don't have to be a dancer, and you don't have to know the way it's going to come out. You need only focus on the question *What is the next smallest step here?* The guidelines are designed to *involve* students, as involvement is the spark that brings the theme to life. In order to develop your own movement activities, ask yourself these questions:

- What is the theme?
- How many small steps can I break this theme into? Or, put another way, how can I structure the environment to generate this response? In what sequence should I introduce the steps? (This step might require some practice and curriculum planning outside of class.)
- Would exaggerating or contrasting work with this theme? (Notice your directions and lean toward vivid descriptive words rather than abstract words. One student was practicing this translation process and was attempting to get his partner to move "aggressively." Both were rather stumped until I asked him to use words that described his actual experience such as *sharp and quick, puffing up,* or *pretending to be an ape meeting a stranger.*)
- What would be a fun part of the body to start with?
- Are my directions clear and specific? (Feel free to write them out at first.)
- Am I letting myself move my body and am I enjoying the activity? (This can be a key in involving the students.)

One alternative is to see if the theme is most involved with moving through time (math), space (proportions, sequences, geography), weight (impact of peer culture, political themes, responsibility), or a combination (science). Then you might choose an activity from the book in that area as part of your curriculum plan for that topic. From that experience you can add to or change parts of a written activity to suit your learning objective.

Several examples of translation follow, to give you an idea of how to design a movement activity from different curriculum themes—character development, understanding idioms, dividing, sequences, and touch. Each example will follow the above steps. When using the translation process, use the number of steps or activities that suit your time frame and the level of development of the topic. You'll have lots of recipes to choose from, and you don't need to cook the whole meal the first time. A five-minute interlude can be more effective than a longer activity if it's carefully and enthusiastically chosen.

CHARACTER DEVELOPMENT

STEPS

a. How do you know the character in this story? How does the character look? Mold your own body into the way you imagine this character appears: tall, short, chunky, skinny, young, old.

b. How does the character stand? Let your body stand in that way.

c. Imagine walking and moving from one place to another the way this character might.

d. Pretend you're another person looking at this character. What do you see?

e. Find a partner and talk to her or him as this character. How does your voice sound? What kind of words do you use?

f. With your eyes closed, travel inside your character and look for his or her feelings. What emotions does your character feel?

g. Let the room represent the whole story, and become your character moving through the action of the story. How do you move: enthusiastically, hesitantly, wanting to go in two or more directions?

h. If this story were a kind of machine, what part would your character be? How does your character help make the story work? (Several characters could actually make a machine.)

METHOD   Exaggerating would work with steps a, b, c, d, g, and h. Contrasting might be fun with e and f.

BODY PARTS   It would probably be easiest to begin with head and hands, adding shoulders and elbows, then feet and knees before moving the whole body.

DIRECTIONS   Take each step you have listed, and write out directions after you answer each question with your own movement and feel the words that are most descriptive for you.

INVOLVEMENT   Intending to let your body movement totally support what you say is the most effortless way to communicate clearly and fully. Then forget about it and focus on the communication itself.

UNDERSTANDING IDIOMS

STEPS

a. Make up your own list of body-related idioms. Some examples might include

keeping an eye on things	butterflies in your
keep a stiff upper lip	stomach
backing down	hard-headed
shouldering the load	cold feet
nose to the grindstone	head over heels
nose in the air	spine of steel
weak-kneed	sharp-tongued
putting your foot in your	
mouth	

b. Have students make up together a list of such idiomatic phrases that they've heard. Explain any unfamiliar phrases.

c. Make another list with more abstract phrases such as

see you around	down in the dumps
all over the place	mad as a hatter
flying apart	letting it all hang out

d. Introduce the idioms in sequence from a to d, with the more concrete, teacher-initiated idioms first.

METHOD Exaggerating works especially well with this theme. An effective sequence is to begin with very exaggerated movement, gradually making it subtler and less obvious until the bridge to verbal content can be easily seen.

BODY PARTS With this theme the key word is *literal*. Acting out each phrase beginning with the part of the body indicated, as with *nose in the air,* and expanding to let the whole body be a nose in the air is great fun for students and can lead them to the body experience underlying the idiom. With the more abstract phrases, notice which area, arms or legs, could most easily move through that phrase. For example, with *down in the dumps,* arms and shoulders could begin to act out the phrase.

DIRECTIONS Writing the phrases on the board as you do them, and having students write out their phrases and their responses in moving would be valuable additions to this activity. You might wish to add the history behind some phrases that are more colorful; for example, years ago, a toxic part of the process of producing hats created a distinct physical and psychological effect on workers that came to be known as being *mad as a hatter.* Examples of the history of phrases can lead students toward understanding the development of language and its roots in experience.

INVOLVEMENT Your movement participation in the beginning of this activity will spark the brainstorming of the students and add levity.

STEPS

a. Smallest step, dividing in half:
   —drawing imaginary line down the midline of your body
   —hands tracing around waist, separating upper and lower body
   —hands clasped, hands apart
   —two students making a circle together with their arms, then stepping back, separating hands but keeping the shape
   —even-numbered group shape of children counting off 1, 2, 1, 2 . . . 1s going to one side of room, 2s to the other, and forming new group shape
   —dividing the room in half, 4s, 8s, by making lines in space with body

b. Dividing by single-digit numbers:
   —moving body parts represent the number to be divided and repeated rhythms signify the divisor. With each group of rhythms (i.e., 3 strong beats), that number of body parts stops moving entirely. How many times can you repeat the rhythm? Do you have any body parts still moving (remainder)?
   —one group of children is the dividend, another the divisor. The divisor comes in, captures their same number, and puts them somewhere else in the room, then comes again and takes another group somewhere else until the dividend group is separated or divided.

METHOD   Contrasting would be a useful underscore to the activity, by having one-half of the group or body moving one quality, the other half its opposite. Moving–not moving, under–over, and so on, are useful contrasts in this activity.

BODY PARTS   In this activity, use the body parts in the various ways they can be divided. Bilateral features would be a good start: two eyes, ears, hands, elbows, knees, feet, and so forth.

DIRECTIONS   Walk through an activity yourself to note any confusion that might be generated by your directions. Feel free to correct and adapt as you go along.

INVOLVEMENT   You might be more the movie director than actor in this activity.

SEQUENCES

STEPS

a. Move up and down very slowly, noticing what makes the next body part move.

b. Do downward swings: starting with head arcs, adding shoulders, then arms, then hanging upper body over, arcing from waist, then swinging whole upper body from hips.

c. Do leg swings: starting with lower leg, gradually larger to include thigh, then large swing from hip, then swing plus hop on opposite leg.

d. Use a gesture, like a shrug or a flick, and have it travel down, through, or across from one side of the body to the other, through the next body part.

e. Do "Dominoes" activity in Chapter 2: each student in turn repeats the same movement with another body part.

f. Do "Telephone," a variation of the activity in Chapter 3: students hold hands seated in circle, eyes closed, and "send" the hand squeeze to the next person in the determined direction.

g. Play river rocks: students pretend to hop from one rock to another in an imaginary river that runs through the room.

METHOD Exaggerating would work well with steps a (exaggerating slowness), b (exaggerating the outbreath as they swing), c. Contrasting qualities would work well with d, e, f, and g, for which exaggeration could be used as well.

BODY PARTS In step a, imagine a weight on the shoulders, making the body sink. In step b, begin with the head. For leg swings, start with strongest leg supporting, the other swinging. Step d can begin with a hand or foot gesture. Dominoes, step e, would be fun to begin with elbows. In "Telephone" begin with a hand squeeze as indicated. Then you might use circling, shaking, raising arms, bringing hands into middle of circle, and so on. For step g, relax, create a river in the imagination first.

DIRECTIONS AND INVOLVEMENT Demonstration is particularly valuable in teaching sequences, which can lead to activities in left–right discrimination, cross-lateral games ("Pease Porridge Hot") and sentence structure, for example. If you demonstrate with voice and movement at the beginning of each activity listed, you may find that the action moves more smoothly.

TOUCH

STEPS

a. Work with phrases about touch:

touchdown	keep in touch
touching performance	I was touched by
touch and go	lost touch with
touchy	out of touch
untouchable	touching on a subject
a light touch	just a touch of spice

b. In a circle of seated students, have each student move around, touching shoulders lightly and then firmly, getting feedback.

c. Create a partner dance with some body part touching partner, and change parts in contact at intervals of a minute or so.

d. Form a group dance with the same instructions as c.

e. Suggest the following partner movement: one seated with eyes closed, the other touching in different ways. The partner whose eyes are closed reacts and gives verbal feedback about preferences. Switch roles.

f. Refer to the sensory awareness activities in the book, which involve touch.

g. Touch others in different roles: as family members, community authorities (clergy, doctor, dentist, etc.).

h. One partner lies down, eyes closed. The other partner touches different body parts lightly and briefly (relaxation: best with music).

METHOD Exaggeration will work very well with step a especially; b is structured as opposites; c and d could use exaggeration; e will have lots of variety and probably should *not* use exaggeration; h should exaggerate light touch.

BODY PARTS Step a would be best to begin this exploration, as touch is a volatile subject and has emotional content for most of us. This exploration could be used to explore students' attitudes about touch before moving to further exploration.

DIRECTIONS The structures for touch activities should be especially direct and clear to provide boundaries.

INVOLVEMENT Your modeling will be valuable to establish ease and comfort in these activities; spend some time exploring your own attitudes about touch so you can be clear in your presentation.

Creative discipline through movement

Discipline problems ideally should not occur in the classroom, which is designed for education, not necessarily mediation—but problems do occur. Students have personality conflicts, unresolved frustrations, difficulties with control of impulses, responses to activities they don't like, peer social needs and demands, uneven development in different areas, and just plain "stuck" places and times. Cultural and environmental influences also impact on students' temperaments: windy days, anticipated holidays, role differentiation, and so on.

Learning problems and discipline problems seem to go hand in hand. When students encounter a problem that is too much for their current resources, they are more likely to retreat to a familiar stress response, two extremes being either a withdrawn, apathetic response or an explosive chaotic response in a difficult learning situation. All of the activities in this book can be viewed as preventive, creating a learning environment that is most likely to be harmonious, well paced, and fun. The following activities are designed more for those breakthrough times when "the best laid plans. . . ."

The emphasis in this section is to develop strategies for discipline problems that increase the student's sense of mastery and self-esteem, assist in resolving the problem, and build bridges for further growth in identified areas.

A Word on Short Interventions

Several activities in this book can be adapted for exploring discipline issues. These are listed in the *Index*. A few additional notes might be useful for your implementation of movement for conflict resolution. The "Flying Free" activity in Chapter 1 can be adapted to interpersonal conflicts by having each person take a position that expresses his or her view of or stand on the situation, then following the remainder of the activity as described. All of the problem-solving activities can be used to shift and expand perspective in a discipline issue, particularly the first variation of "Sea Trees" in Chapter 6.

Impulse control is a problem that teachers mention often in discussions of major discipline issues. A short intervention that can be very effective, especially for angry outbursts, is to have the students imagine that the thing they are upset about is out in front of them, making it even bigger. Then, taking a huge breath, they can blow it over, out of the room, against the wall, whatever. Usually two or three blowouts will defuse the impulse. Walking backwards will also create the same effect, and teachers have used this intervention on the playground as well as in the classroom. For example, when two students come running up yelling "He hit me"; "Well, he called me a name!", the teacher can respond, "Okay, Bill and Charlie, I want you to walk backwards all the way to that tree and then come back and we'll talk." By the time they've walked backwards, the initial disturbance most often dissolves.

Some quick interventions in the initial phase of the problem can often defuse and actually transform the interaction. Acknowledging another person's feelings is a key step. Completing the phrase, "Right now I feel _____" in movement several times in succession with adversaries exchanging active and listening roles is fundamental to shifting from a stuck place. Learning to listen is a difficult and essential part of growing up and a skill that this brief interchange can develop. Teachers have mentioned projection as a major issue in discipline, the student's view that everything is someone else's fault. This short activity emphasizes response-ability for one's feelings, as do subsequent experiments. We recommend it as an introduction to any of the following activities.

ECHOES

TO THE LEADER   How would you feel if you were the other person? The answer to this question is part of critical learning skills and also essential to conflict resolution. This experiment gives the participants an active chance to walk in another's shoes. It's easiest to introduce in partners, and can also be used in a group to follow one leader.

INSTRUCTIONS TO THE GROUP   Pair up and find some open space in the room. Partner One, begin walking through the room in your most familiar walk, striding out just the way you feel right now . . . great. Now Partner Two, your job is to echo Partner One's walk. Walk right behind your partner and take some time to let your head, shoulders, elbows, hips, knees, and feet move just the way Partner One's do. How fast or slowly is your partner walking? How big is the stride? How does the weight shift from one foot to the other? Take some time to study your partner's walk.

(1–3 minutes.)

When you feel you've got it, signal your partner so he or she can stop walking and watch you being the echo.
Now switch. Partner Two, you walk the way you're feeling right now, and Partner One, you begin to echo your partner's walk.

(Repeat some of above questions.)

VARIATION   In addition to echoing their partners' walks, have the students hum to themselves the rhythm and tone of the walk. They can often discover new qualities of movement by finding the hum that fits.

THE RUMBLE

TO THE LEADER Sometimes pushing up against another person seems inevitable. This activity is designed for the two students who always end up in the corner punching it out. You'll probably find that many students want to play this game. The structure is very important in this activity, as is *agreement* to follow the rules. You'll be the referee. Fight music such as "The Rumble" from *West Side Story* is evocative and also establishes the activity as ritual or drama.

INSTRUCTIONS TO THE GROUP   Okay, everyone who wants to rumble, gather over here. These are the rules: (1) No touching. You'll need to be very alert so you can help your partner with this one. Anyone who touches is out. (2) Each person takes a turn. One person gets to take a swing at the other, and that person has to fall down. Then the faller gets to take a swing, and the other person falls down. Back and forth, as many times as you like (*or you structure, perhaps four turns each*). (3) Move in slow motion. You're going to make your swings as puffed up as you want, like karate or boxing or whatever, but you must swing in slow motion, as though you were underwater. (4) Go one pair at a time. The rest of you will watch and help by actively being present for the two who are rumbling. Any questions? All right, who wants to be first?

COMMENT   You may need to demonstrate with a partner the process of responding to another's swing or push, so that participants understand that half the game is being closely aware of their partner's movement.

128

UNDERWORDS

TO THE LEADER   In a conflict, words can sometimes create an endless circle of blame and rejoinder. This simple activity is useful in such an impasse and can be interjected into daily activities without preparation or a change of setting.

INSTRUCTIONS TO THE GROUP   Let's continue what we're saying, but without using words. Take turns making a statement, expressing whatever you're feeling about this, your viewpoint, the way you see it. But let your *body* say it . . . no words. When your partner is moving, use your whole body to listen and respond. Wait for a nonverbal signal from your partner to make your next statement.

(Continue for 1–3 minutes.)

VARIATION   Conduct the "conversation" with crayons or pastels on large butcher paper or newspaper end rolls, encouraging participants to let the whole body move as they make their statements on paper.

IN AND OUT

TO THE LEADER   This activity is for the individual student, and several students or the whole classroom can participate simultaneously. This experiment is useful for times when a student feels cornered or boxed in by a situation. To create a situation where the solution is internally generated can build an increased sense of self-esteem and inner control.

INSTRUCTIONS TO THE GROUP   Move quickly to a place in the room where you have just the right amount of space around you. Good. Close your eyes and let yourself breathe into the space around you for a moment. Pretend that this thing you're dealing with right now has an actual shape and size. Let it become a form all around you. Let your hands reach out and explore this thing. Notice what texture it has . . . rough, ripply, smooth. How close to your body is it? Can you stand up?

(Continue for 30–60 seconds.)

Now, keeping your eyes closed, can you find or create some kind of opening to get out of this shape? Imagine just the perfect way out for you right now. And get out!

(30–60 seconds.)

Great . . . now that you're out, what would you like to do with this shape? Let's take a few minutes to share our experiences.

COMMENT   There's a possibility that a student might not readily find an opening. You can ask what assistance she or he needs, a helper or wizard or parent or ladder, then invite that student to imagine the helper in the shape with her or him.

References

Publications

American Journal of Dance Therapy. American Dance Therapy Association, 2000 Century Plaza, Columbia, Maryland 21044.

Andrew, Gladys. *Creative Rhythmic Movement for Children*. Englewood Cliffs, NJ: Prentice-Hall, 1954.

The Annotated Mother Goose. Introduction by William Baring-Gould and Ceil Baring-Gould. New York: Bramhall House, 1962.

Ayres, A. Jean. *Sensory Integration and the Child*. Los Angeles: Western Psychological Services, 1979.

Barlin, Anne Lief. *Teaching Your Wings to Fly*. Santa Monica, CA: Goodyear Publishing Company, 1979.

Barlin, Anne and Paul Barlin. *The Art of Learning Through Movement*. Dublin, Ireland: Ward River Press, 1971.

Barlin, Anne and T. Greenberg. *Move and Be Moved*. Los Angeles:

References

Learning Through Movement, 5757 Ranchito, Van Nuys, CA 94401.

Bernstein, Penny (Ed.). *Eight Theoretical Approaches in Dance-Movement Therapy*. Iowa: Kendall-Hunt, 1979.

Boorman, Joyce. *Creative Dance in the First Three Grades*. New York: David McKay Co., 1969.

Canner, Norma and Harriet Klebanoff. *And a Time to Dance*. Boston: Beacon Press, 1968.

Cherry, Clare. *Creative Movement for the Developing Child*. Palo Alto: Pitman Learning, 1968.

The Complete Grimm's Fairy Tales. New York: Pantheon, 1944, 1972.

Dell, Cecily. *A Primer for Movement Description*. New York: Dance Notation Bureau, 1970.

Durckheim, Karlfried. *Hara: the Vital Centre of Man*. New York: Samuel Weiser, 1975.

Dychtwald, Ken. *Bodymind*. New York: Jove, 1977.

Gendlin, Eugene. *Focusing*. New York: Everest House, 1978.

Hanna, Thomas. *The Body of Life*. New York: Alfred A. Knopf, 1980.

Hendricks, Gay and R. Wills. *The Centering Book*. Englewood Cliffs, NJ: Prentice-Hall, 1975.

Hendricks, Gay. *The Family Centering Book*. Englewood Cliffs, NJ: Prentice-Hall, 1979.

Hendricks, Gay. *The Centered Teacher*. Englewood Cliffs, NJ: Prentice-Hall, 1981.

Hendricks, Gay and T. Roberts. *The Second Centering Book*. Englewood Cliffs, NJ: Prentice-Hall, 1977.

Hendricks, Gay and B. Weinhold. *Transpersonal Approaches to Counseling and Psychotherapy*. Denver: Love Publishing Co., 1982.

Hendricks, Gay. *Learning To Love Yourself*. Englewood Cliffs, NJ: Prentice-Hall, 1982.

Hendricks, Kathlyn. "Transpersonal Movement Therapy," in *Transpersonal Approaches to Counseling and Psychotherapy*, Hendricks and Weinhold. Denver: Love Publishing Co., 1982.

132

Huang, Al. *Embrace Tiger, Return to Mountain*. Moab, Utah: Real People Press, 1973.

Kurtz, Ron and Hector Prestera. *The Body Reveals*. New York: Harper and Row, 1976.

Lamb, Warren and E. Watson. *Body Code: The Meaning in Movement*. London: Routledge, Kegan Paul, 1979.

Leonard, George. *The Silent Pulse*. New York: Dutton, 1978.

Lowen, Alexander. *Bioenergetics*. New York: Penguin, 1974.

Mettler, Barbara. *Materials of Dance As a Creative Art Activity*. Tucson: Mettler Studios, 1960.

Morris, Desmond. *Manwatching*. New York: Harry Abrams, 1977.

Preston, Valerie. *A Handbook for Modern Educational Dance*. New York: Dance Notation Bureau, 1969.

Sweigard, Lulu. *Human Movement Potential*. New York: Harper and Row, 1974.

Wosien, Maria-Gabrile. *Sacred Dance*. New York: Avon, 1974.

Music Reference List

The following selections have all been used successfully with movement activities. We have grouped them in general categories for easier selection. Music provides a definite structure that you might or might not want for a particular activity. We recommend that you personally investigate musical selections and become familiar with each before introducing it in an activity. This list is by no means inclusive, but does contain our favorites.

RELAXATION MUSIC

"Environments" Records: Syntonic Research Series.

Steven Halpern's recordings: SRI Research, 321 Emerson, Palo Alto, CA 94301.

"Music for Zen Meditation," V/V6-8634.

"Lullaby from the Womb," Capitol, ST-11421.

William Ackerman's guitar music, Windham Hill Records, Box 9388, Stanford, CA 94305.

Paul Horn, "Inside," BXN 26466 and "Inside II," KE 31600.

References

"The Koto Music of Japan," Nonesuch HS-72005.

Kitaro's music: "Silk Road," "Oasis," "Ki."

Larkin, "O'cean."

Zamfir, "Solitude," Mercury 7200238.

"Mother Earth's Lullaby," Synchestra.

Brian Eno, "Ambient I" PVC 7908 and "Ambient II," EGS 202 EGS 202Z.

Alan Stivell, "Renaissance of the Celtic Harp," Philips 6414 406.

"Seapeace," Georgia Kelly, P. O. Box 954, Topanga, CA 90290.

EMOTIONALLY EVOCATIVE MUSIC

"Tibetan Bells," Antilles Records AN-7006.

"Heaven and Hell," Vangelis, ATL1-5110.

Samuel Barber, "Adagio for Strings."

Moussorgsky, "Night on Bald Mountain."

"State of Siege," Columbia S 32352.

Paul Winter, "Callings."

"Music for 18 Musician," Steve Reich, ECM1-1129.

Keith Jarrett, "The Koln Concert," ECM 1064/65 ST.

Vangelis, "Chariots of Fire," Polygram PD-1-6335.

Vangelis, "Opera Savage," Polydor 2490-161.

Carl Orff, "Carmina Burana."

Holst, "The Planets."

"Rodrigo: Concierto de Aranjuez."

JOURNEY MUSIC

Moussorgsky, "Pictures at an Exhibition."

Smetana, "The Moldau."

The Beatles, "Yellow Submarine," instrumental side.

Ron Dexter, "Golden Voyage."

Hovhaness, "Mysterious Mountain."

Vaughan Williams, "Fantasia on a Theme by Thomas Tallis."

Handel, "Watermusick."

ETHNIC MUSIC

H. Aram Gulezyan, "The Oud," LLST-7160.

"Hora," *Songs and Dances of Israel,* Elektra EKL-7186.

References

"Hi Neighbors," *Songs and Dances of Brazil, Israel, Ghana, Japan, Turkey,* CMS UNICEF 2.

Ravi Shankar, "Ragas and Tālas," World Pacific, 1431.

Manos Hadjidakis, "Lilacs Out of the Dead Land," PI-LPS-11.

"Rhythms of the World," narrated by Langston Hughes, Folkways, FP 740.

Preservation Hall Jazz Band, New Orleans Jazz.

"Mountain Music Bluegrass Style," Folkways Records, FA 2318.

"Fiestas of Peru," Nonesuch, H-72045.

Elizabeth Waldo, "Realm of the Incas," GNP 603.

"Music for Belly Dancing," Monitor MFS 740.

John McCutcheon, "The Wind that Shakes the Barley," JA 014.

GROUP INTERACTION MUSIC

"Festival Folk Dances," *Michael Hermen's Folk Dance Orchestra,* RCA LPM-1621.

"The Whole World Dances," EKS-7206.

"Missa Luba," Philips PCC 606.

Scott Joplin's music.

Olatunji, "Drums of Passion," CS 8210.

"Irish Jigs, Reels and Hornpipes," Folkways, FP 818/2.

Hap Palmer, "Modern Tunes for Rhythms and Instruments" and "Moving," Educational Activities, Box 392, Freeport, New York 11520.

"Paul Horn and Nexus," Epic, KE 33561.

Brian Eno-David Byrne, "My Life in the Bush of Ghosts," Sire Records, SRK 6093.

Soundtrack from "The Sting."

Cat Stevens, "Teaser and the Firecat," A & M ST 4313.

Michael Jarre, "Exquinoxe" and "Oxygene," Polydor PD-1-6175 (Equinoxe) and PD-1-6112 (Oxygene).

Jimmy Cliff, "The Harder They Come," MLPS-9202.

Marlo Thomas, "Free to Be You and Me," Arista 4003.

CLASSICAL MUSIC

Zabaleta, "Harp Music of the Renaissance," Everest 3340.

"Notturno," Stereolab USD-2126.

References

Vivaldi, *Six Concerti for Flute, Strings and Continuo, Op. 10,* Nonesuch H-71042.

Kranis, "The Virtuoso Recorder": from *Folk Dances to Blues,* Odyssey—32 160143.

Bach, "Brandenburg Concertos."

Pachelbel, "Canon in D."

"Faure Requiem" Op. 90.

"Greatest Hits of 1720 and 1721," CBS Masterworks MX34544 and M35821.

MISCELLANEOUS

"Music for Movement" and "Basic Rhythms," Set No. 1, Kay Ortmans Productions, 2005 Alba Rd., Ben Lomond, CA 95005.

"Dance-a-Long," Folkways Record, RC 7651.

Anne Barlin's work, including "Dance-A-Story," "Cloud Journeys," and films; available from Learning Through Movement, 5757 Ranchito, Van Nuys, CA 91401.

Index

Index

Index

NOW ... Announcing these other fine books from Prentice-Hall—

OUR CLASSROOM: We Can Learn Together by Chick Moorman and Dee Dishon. This book offers specific ideas, techniques, and strategies for creating the kind of cooperative community environment that eliminates discipline and apathy problems—and makes students eager to learn and participate. Directed at K–6 teachers, it covers managing the classroom for control and cooperation, inviting student input and responsibility, acting as role model, and more.

$6.95 paperback, $14.95 hardcover

THE CENTERED TEACHER: Awareness Activities for Teachers and Their Students by Gay Hendricks. Provides an entire new curriculum with more than 60 mind–body activities plus specific how-to-do-it instructions that teachers need to successfully incorporate centered activities into their daily classroom schedules.

$5.95 paperback, $11.95 hardcover

To order these books, just complete the convenient order form below and mail to Prentice-Hall, Inc., General Publishing Division, Attn. Addison Tredd, Englewood Cliffs, N.J. 07632

Title	Author	Price*

Subtotal _____

Sales Tax (where applicable) _____

Postage & Handling (75¢/book) _____

Total $ _____

Please send me the books listed above. Enclosed is my check ☐ Money order ☐ or, charge my VISA ☐ MasterCard ☐ Account # _____

Credit card expiration date _____

Name _____

Address _____

City _____ State _____ Zip _____

Prices subject to change without notice. Please allow 4 weeks for delivery.